THE WANNABE MINUTE MASTER

THE WANNABE MINUTE MASTER
30 Steps to Become Time Affluent

ANN MARIE SABATH

SONCATA PRESS

NEW YORK, NEW YORK

Hardback ISBN: 979-89908510-8-5
Paperback ISBN: 979-8-9926452-0-0
ebook ISBN: 979-8-9926452-1-7
Audiobook ISBN: 979-8-9926452-2-4

Library of Congress Control Number: 2025935933

Cover design by Howard Grossman.

Attention Educational Institutions and Businesses:
Soncata Press books are available at special quantity discounts with bulk purchase for educational, business, or sales promotional use. For information, please write to contact@soncatapress.com.

*To Elliott, whose entrepreneurial mindset led to
the creation of* The Wannabe *series. Thank you for seeing
the bigger picture before anyone else did.*

Contents

INTRODUCTION
The Global Time Crunch

*Time is the coin of your life. It is the only coin you have, and only
you can determine how it will be spent. Be careful lest you let
other people spend it for you.*

CARL SANDBURG

Have you ever caught yourself saying "There just aren't enough hours in the day"? You're not the only one. Across countries and cultures, from bustling cities to quieter towns, people everywhere are feeling the pressure of time—or, more precisely, the lack of it. It's not just a packed schedule or a long to-do list. It is the deeper frustration of wanting more time for what matters most—and not knowing how to find it.

In fact, the 2024 Workforce Wellness Report by FlexJobs found that more than 70 percent of the 3,000 US-based employees surveyed said companies should reconsider their workweeks. A large majority (89 percent of respondents) were in favor of modifications, with 32 percent supporting shorter workweeks, 32 percent flexible schedules, and 25 percent performance-based arrangements in which hours are based on goals. Experts say that changes to the traditional workweek, which often help with retention and combatting burnout, were differentiators in the recruiting process.

After pilot projects in 2015 and 2019, Iceland made four-day workweeks standard. In fact, 97 percent of the workers who received shorter hours agreed that it made it easier to balance work with their private lives, with 42 percent sharing that it had decreased their stress.[1]

Around the world, people are feeling stretched thin. They're craving more time to spend with loved ones, to move their bodies, to create, rest, travel, or simply breathe. But the problem is not just about having too much to do. It is about how we relate to time. We often treat it as something to chase, conquer, or squeeze into tighter margins. In doing so, we forget that time is not just a resource—it reflects what we value.

Time Affluence: The New Definition of Wealth

This book is about reclaiming that value. It's about something called *time affluence*—the feeling that you have enough time for the things that make life meaningful.

Not surprisingly, feeling time-poor has real consequences. A growing body of research suggests that when we feel like we are always rushing or behind, our mental health suffers, our relationships weaken, and our creativity fades. Even basic self-care takes a back seat. According to *TIME* magazine, time scarcity can lead to a host of negative ripple effects: poorer sleep, reduced exercise, and even more impulsive decision-making.[2] It is not just stressful—it is unsustainable.

The good news? You do not have to overhaul your life or become a minimalist monk to feel more in control of your time. What you do need is a mindset shift—paired with a few practical strategies to protect your minutes from being swallowed up by everything that does not serve you.

A Global Guide for the Time-Strapped

No matter where you live or what you do for a living, time affluence is within reach. This book was written with a global reader in mind—

whether you're managing a busy household in Jakarta, running a startup in Berlin, freelancing in Nairobi, or navigating remote work in São Paulo.

Inside these pages are 30 simple steps—each one designed to help you gently take your time back. Some are mindset tweaks. Others are daily practices. All are bite-sized and actionable, so you can begin wherever you are, without needing to pause your life to implement them. Because time affluence isn't about doing less—it's about doing more of what matters.

So, take a breath. Open to any page. Try one idea. Then another.

Let this be the moment you start making time for the life you want—not someday, but now.

How This Book Is Organized

The Wannabe Minute Master is divided into seven sections that describe 30 steps to time affluence.

PART 1: UNDERSTAND YOUR RELATIONSHIP WITH TIME

Step 1: Understand How You Value Time. In this step, you will explore your unique definition of time affluence. You will also have a chance to assess how your existing lifestyle aligns with your goals and values.

Step 2: Identify Your Time Personality. This engaging quiz has been created to help to uncover your time management style. It is meant to be a starting point for your time-affluent growth.

PART 2: BUILD THE FOUNDATION FOR TIME AFFLUENCE

Step 3: Identify Your Most Productive Time of Day. This step is meant to help you define your peak productivity hours. By doing so, you will be able to maximize efficiency for your high-priority tasks.

Step 4: Schedule a Minimum of 2 Hours of Free Time Each Day. In this step, you are encouraged to carve out personal time to recharge and focus on your well-being.

Step 5: Create a Customized Time Budget. This step is to help allocate your time with intention. You will find it to be much like a financial budget—to ensure your priorities are aligned with your goals.

Step 6: Be Mindful of Your Minutes. In this step, you are encouraged to track and reflect on how they spend your time, identifying and minimizing wasteful habits.

Step 7: Be Respectful of Others' Time. This step highlights the importance of fostering mutual respect for time in personal and professional relationships through clear boundaries and expectations.

PART 3: PLAN AND PRIORITIZE FOR DAILY SUCCESS

Step 8: Create a Daily Routine. This step introduces the power of habits and structure to bring consistency and balance to daily life.

Step 9: Plan Your Day the Night Before. This step demonstrates how prior planning can set the stage for a focused and productive day.

Step 10: Integrate Habit Stacking into Your Life. This step teaches how to build new habits by pairing them with existing ones for efficiency and consistency.

Step 11: Create a Daily To-Do List. This step emphasizes the benefits of prioritizing tasks with a simple, structured list.

Step 12: Have a Running To-Do List. This step emphasizes maintaining an ongoing list to help organize tasks and prevent important items from slipping through the cracks.

PART 4: PRACTICE EFFECTIVE TIME MANAGEMENT STRATEGIES

Step 13: Eat That Frog! This classic strategy teaches you to tackle your hardest tasks first for a sense of accomplishment and momentum.

Step 14: Touch It Once! This step explores the efficiency of addressing tasks immediately to avoid procrastination and duplication of effort.

Step 15: The 2-Minute Rule: Do It Now! In this step, you learn to handle small tasks on the spot, reducing mental clutter and freeing up time for larger priorities.

Step 16: Stay Focused. This step shares strategies for minimizing distractions and maintaining concentration.

Step 17: Set Boundaries. In this step, you are guided on how to protect your time by setting clear limits with others.

Step 18: Use Meeting Agendas. This step emphasizes the importance of preparation and structure for effective meetings.

PART 5: MAXIMIZE TIME AND TECHNOLOGY

Step 19: Stop Time-Leaking Conversations. This step explores how to identify and address unproductive conversations to protect your time and energy.

Step 20: Minimize Wait Time. This step explores strategies for reducing unnecessary delays and downtime.

Step 21: Leverage Dead Time. In this step, you learn to make use of idle moments, such as commuting or waiting, to accomplish small tasks or reflect on goals.

Step 22: Use Digital Technology to Your Advantage. This step provides tips on using apps and tools to streamline tasks and become more productive.

PART 6: SIMPLIFY AND STREAMLINE LIFE

Step 23: Minimize Decision Fatigue. In this step, you learn how making small decisions depletes mental energy and productivity, and you gain ideas for streamlining decision-making.

Step 24: Declutter Your Space. This step explores the connection between mental clarity and a clean, organized environment.

Step 25: Streamline Your Dressing Routine. In this step, you learn how simplifying daily clothing choices can save time and reduce stress.

Step 26: Turn Off Default Notifications. In this step, you are encouraged to eliminate unnecessary digital distractions by managing your device settings.

Step 27: Unplug from Technology. This step emphasizes the importance of periodically disconnecting from technology to recharge and reconnect with life.

Step 28: Set Tech-Free Zones at Home and at Work. This step explores strategies for creating distraction-free spaces to foster focus and relaxation.

PART 7: BUILD TIME AFFLUENCE FOR LIFE

Step 29: Learn to Deal with Setbacks. In this step, you learn strategies for recovering from time management setbacks, reflecting on lessons, and regaining momentum.

Step 30: Be Available for What (and Who) Matters Most. In this final step, you reconnect with the *reason* you are pursuing time affluence.

The book concludes with a reflection on your journey toward time affluence, encouraging you to apply what you've learned to live intentionally and achieve lasting fulfillment.

Reading this book is one thing. Putting into practice one or more of the steps to time affluence will be the secret sauce for giving yourself more time. To assist you in doing so, at the end of this book you will find companion exercises for each of the 30 steps. They are meant to give you simple ways of creating new time efficiency habits.

Ready, set, go!

PART 1

Understand Your Relationship with Time

STEP 1
Understand How You Value Time

Time is more valuable than money. You can get more money,
but you cannot get more time.
JIM ROHN, AMERICAN ENTREPRENEUR

———————

Have you ever put a value on an hour of your time? While I've worked with clients who billed their time hourly, it rarely occurred to me to put a dollar value on my own time—until I began writing this book.

Growing up, I often heard the phrase "Time is money," but I never truly reflected on its meaning. When I began viewing each day's 24 hours through a monetary lens, I realized I had always placed a higher value on my salary than on the actual hours in my day. Supporting a family was my top priority, and assigning a value to my time wasn't something I even considered.

So, let me ask you: If you were to put a dollar figure on each hour in your day, what would it be? $100? $200? $300?

What Americans Think Their Time Is Worth

A 2024 survey by Empower, a financial planning firm, asked 2,204 adults to assign a monetary value to an hour of their time. The average answer was $240/hour.[3]

Let's put that in perspective: $240/hour × 40 hours/week × 52 weeks/year = $499,200 annually. That's eight times the average US salary in the first quarter of 2025, which was $62,088.

The survey revealed intriguing generational differences in how people value their time:

- Gen Z (1997–2012): Average value = $266.92/hour
- Millennials (1981–1996): Average value = $328.84/hour (and 25 percent valued their time at $500/hour or more!)
- Gen X (1965–1980): Average value = $125.90/hour
- Boomers (1946–1964): Average value = $137.19/hour

The survey also revealed what truly makes people feel wealthy:

- 63 percent said having enough time to spend with family and friends made them feel rich.
- 40 percent valued saving time over having money, with 52 percent of millennials sharing this sentiment.

Why do so many people value time over money? The answer is simple: Time is a nonrenewable resource. Unlike money, which can be earned and replenished, time is finite. Once it's spent, it's gone forever.

Could it be that many people learned this lesson the hard way? Missing a loved one's special event, prioritizing work over personal connections, or letting relationships falter often leads to regret—and a deeper appreciation for the value of time.

What about you? Do you place a higher value on making money or having more personal time?

Quiz: Do You Value More Time or More Money?

Take this quick quiz to discover what you prioritize most!

DIRECTIONS
Circle the letter that best reflects your perspective.

1. How do you feel after a busy workweek?
   A. I wish I had more time to relax and connect with loved ones.
   B. I feel accomplished and excited about the money I earned.

2. Imagine your perfect weekend:
   A. Spending quality time with family and friends or enjoying hobbies.
   B. Being productive, like studying or pursuing extra income opportunities.

3. If offered a job that pays double but requires extensive travel, would you take it?
   A. No, I prefer work-life balance.
   B. Yes, the extra money is worth it.

4. How do you decide how to spend your free time?
   A. I prioritize meaningful time with loved ones.
   B. I focus on activities that could lead to financial gain.

5. At the end of your life, what would make you feel most fulfilled?
   A. Knowing I spent quality time with loved ones.
   B. Knowing I achieved financial success.

HOW DID YOU SCORE?

If you circled mostly A's, you value personal time and recognize its irreplaceable nature. Family, friends, and meaningful experiences are your priorities.

If you circled mostly B's, financial success drives you, and you're willing to trade personal time to achieve it.

Your Call to Action

Take a moment today to put a dollar figure on 1 hour of your time—not based on your salary, but on what your time is truly worth to you. Ask yourself what you'd be willing to pay for 1 uninterrupted hour with someone you love, or for time to do something that brings you joy. When you start valuing your time like the limited resource it is, your priorities begin to shift—toward what matters most. So, before you dive into the rest of this book, anchor yourself with this truth: Your time is valuable, and how you spend it is your most powerful choice.

TIME AFFLUENCE TIP FROM A TOP CEO

Naval Ravikant, co-founder, chairman, and former CEO of AngelList advocates that individuals set an aspirational hourly rate to put the value of their time in perspective.[4] For him, it was $5,000 per hour (he's not joking about the aspirational part!); for you, it might be different. Once you have an aspirational value of your time, though, it helps put things on your schedule into a bit more perspective. If you value your time at $5,000 per hour as Ravikant did, or even at $250 like many of us might, then it becomes very easy to justify paying for a service to save you a couple of hours of time and help free up your schedule.

STEP 2
Identify Your Time Personality

Personality is to a man what perfume is to a flower.
CHARLES SCHWAB

———————
———————

People have different approaches to time based on their goals, upbringing, and personal values. Some prioritize efficiency and productivity, structuring their days around maximizing output. Others see time as something to be enjoyed, prioritizing experiences, relationships, and personal well-being. There's no single way to view time, but understanding your own tendencies and those of the people around you can help you make better decisions and strike a balance that aligns with your priorities.

Quiz: Identify Your Time Personality

Take this quiz to learn your time personality so you can capitalize on your strengths and tackle future time challenges more effectively.

DIRECTIONS
Circle the letter that best reflects your perspective.

1. How do you typically handle your to-do list?
   A. I tend to put things off until necessary.
   B. I like to juggle multiple tasks at the same time.
   C. I carefully organize and prioritize everything on my list.
   D. A to-do list? I just deal with things as they arise.

2. What's your take on deadlines?
   A. I enjoy the rush of working under last-minute pressure.
   B. I find myself often losing focus and missing them.
   C. I prepare in advance and meet my deadlines.
   D. Deadlines can be frustrating since they interrupt my flow.

3. How do you usually feel at the end of the day?
   A. Just relieved to have made it through (barely).
   B. Overwhelmed by all the tasks I did not complete.
   C. Proud and satisfied with what I accomplished.
   D. Tired, but I did what felt right in the moment.

4. When working on a project, what is your usual method?
   A. I wait until the last moment to start working on it.
   B. I work on it in between my other tasks.
   C. I plan out every part of the project before I start.
   D. I complete it in the way that I feel is best.

5. How do you feel about new tasks being added to your plate?
   A. I dislike it when others add things for me to do.
   B. I usually like it since I can just do all of it at once.
   C. I don't usually mind, but sometimes I get a little overwhelmed.
   D. I just do them after I finish what I was already doing.

6. What's your attitude toward breaks?
    A. I don't take breaks; I just keep working.
    B. I take a range of breaks while working.
    C. I take breaks after I finish a task.
    D. I take breaks if I feel like I need one.

7. How do you view your limits?
    A. I don't have limits; I just keep pushing myself until I get it all done.
    B. I don't know where my limits are, but I'm going to do my best.
    C. I know my limits and know when to stop or ask for help.
    D. I know where my limits are, but I still push myself to go beyond them.

8. What do you think your time style is?
    A. I am someone who tries to do everything at once.
    B. I am someone who takes a little bit of time to get done all I can.
    C. I am someone who takes their time on all they do.
    D. I am someone who just does what needs to be done.

9. When you finish working, how do you feel?
    A. I feel like I did everything I could.
    B. I feel like I did a decent job.
    C. I feel like I could have done better.
    D. I feel like I'm going to do it again later.

10. How do you feel about planning?
    A. I don't like planning; I just do things in the moment.
    B. I like planning, but it doesn't mean I will follow the plan.
    C. I like to plan but not too much.
    D. I do not like to plan everything.

HOW DID YOU SCORE?

Now that you have completed the quiz, let's assess your time personality style.

If you circled mostly A's, you might be a **procrastinator** who does well when there's pressure yet has trouble starting tasks. To improve, try breaking projects into smaller, manageable steps and setting mini deadlines to ease last-minute stress.

If you chose mostly B's, you could be a **multitasker** handling various responsibilities, which can be overwhelming at times. Try to focus on one task at a time and organize your to-do list to take back control of your schedule.

If you marked mostly C's, you are probably a **planner**—organized and efficient, but possibly a bit too rigid. To prevent burnout, make sure to include some flexibility and spontaneity in your routine.

If you circled mostly D's, you might be an **improvisor** who enjoys spontaneity, which can create some chaos. To find a better balance between freedom and productivity, consider adding more structure to your daily activities.

By recognizing your time management style, you may better recognize the steps in *The Wannabe Minute Master* that will most benefit you!

Your Call to Action

Review your answers to the quiz in this chapter. What patterns do you notice in your answers? How do these responses reflect your current time management style?

No matter your results, you now have the power to consciously evaluate how you value your time. Start with one small action: Look for one activity you can delegate or decline this week. Use that time to do something meaningful, and see how it feels to take control of your most precious resource.

TIME AFFLUENCE TIP FROM A TOP CEO

One notable multitasker is Stephen Carter, former CEO of Cingular Wireless. Carter managed his demanding role by establishing strict operational rules and leveraging technology to stay organized. He handled about 200 emails daily and spent significant time traveling, yet maintained a sense of calm and control through disciplined multi-tasking practices. His approach exemplifies how structured multitasking can be effectively implemented at the executive level.[5]

PART 2

Build the Foundation for Time Affluence

STEP 3
Identify Your Most Productive Time of Day

*Productivity is never an accident. It is always the result of a
commitment to excellence, intelligent planning, and focused effort.*
**PAUL J. MEYER, AUTHOR OF *FORTUNE, FAMILY & FAITH* AND
*UNLOCKING YOUR LEGACY***

———————

What would you say is your most productive time of day? Are you at your
sharpest in the early morning or late afternoon? Or does your creativity
peak in the early evening—or perhaps even in the middle of the night?

When I wrote this question, I also posed it to myself. I glanced at the
clock, and it was 10:29 p.m.—so the answer was clear! My peak energy
and alertness usually kick in during the late evening and into the early
morning hours.

If you're unsure when your peak productivity strikes, take a few
moments to answer these questions:

- When are you able to concentrate on your most challenging tasks?
- When do you feel the most sluggish, as if you need a power nap?
- What time of day do you prefer to schedule important meetings
  or presentations?

Now that you've reflected on these questions, let's assess your peak
performance times. As Christopher M. Barnes explains in his personal
productivity article for the *Harvard Business Review*, understanding your

circadian rhythms can help you align your work with your natural energy cycles.[6]

Morning: If you find yourself most productive between 6:00 a.m. and 11:00 a.m., you're likely a morning lark. This suggests you should tackle the day's most demanding tasks first. Your decision-making and problem-solving abilities are probably strongest in the morning. If mornings aren't your peak time and you need to warm up throughout the day, focus on routine tasks in the early hours and save the heavier work for later.

Afternoon: If you feel most energized from noon to 4:00 p.m., you may experience a midday peak. Your energy builds as the day progresses. However, if you notice a dip in the afternoon, consider taking a 30-minute power nap. If that's not feasible at work, adjust your schedule to handle lighter tasks during this low-alertness period. And who knows—if you forward your boss Barnes's article, maybe they'll see the value of afternoon naps too!

Evening/Night: If you're most productive during the evening or after the clock strikes midnight, join the club! I've learned to cherish these hours when "not a creature was [supposed to be] stirring, not even a mouse." (I did have an encounter with a mouse in the wee writing hours once—and I was wide awake after that, for sure!) Rather than fight your tendency, embrace it. If you are most creative when the world quiets down, just think: You will have fewer distractions, fewer emails, and a sense of calm that may allow you to concentrate. If this describes your natural energy level, schedule projects that require deep thinking or problem-solving for late night. When possible, structure your day to accommodate this rhythm by starting later in the morning or building in time for that power nap during the afternoon. (Oh no, I'm giving away my secrets!)

Your Call to Action

To identify your peak productivity windows, observe trends in your daily energy cycles. First, track your energy levels for three consecutive days.

Use a simple chart or journal to record your focus, alertness, and mood at regular intervals (say, every 2 hours). Note the tasks you were working on and how well you performed them. Then, reflect on your findings: When were you the most focused? When did you feel the most distracted or sluggish? Did any patterns emerge across the three days?

TIME AFFLUENCE TIP FROM A TOP CEO

Tim Cook, CEO of Apple, wakes up at 3:45 every morning, does email for an hour, then goes to the gym; then Starbucks for more email, then work. He says, "The thing about it is, when you love what you do, you don't really think of it as work. It's what you do. And that's the good fortune of where I find myself."[7]

———————
———————

STEP 4
Schedule a Minimum of 2 Hours of Free Time Each Day

*Do not let a day go by without taking time for yourself—some
time you spend in pure pleasure, as you see it.*
NAPOLEON HILL

Acquiring a time-affluent mindset starts with making time for yourself. No matter how many time management techniques you use, it's essential to prioritize yourself. The greatest gift you can give is that of time—time for yourself. If you're skeptical, keep reading.

How Many Hours of Daily Free Time Do You Need?

Research shows that having between 2 and 5 hours of free time each day is crucial not only for feeling but for *being* time-affluent. The perception of having at least 120 minutes each day solely for yourself gives you a sense of control. Whether you spend that time walking, napping, or socializing, the key is that it's time you've intentionally dedicated to your well-being. Treating this time as a necessity rather than a luxury is vital. Just as drinking water keeps you hydrated, carving out time for yourself keeps you balanced and productive. By setting aside a couple of hours each day, you'll find greater joy, relaxation, and personal growth, leading to increased satisfaction in life.

A 2023 article in *Psychology Today* cites a study by Sharif, Mogilner, and Hershfield that found having less than 2 hours of free time per day leads to stress, while more than 5 hours can result in feelings of unproductivity and unhappiness.[8]

Reflecting on my own experiences, I used to feel guilty about carving out time for myself. I stopped feeling guilty when I realized that my disposition was much better when I created "me time"—having an uninterrupted telephone conversation with a friend, reading, or simply relaxing—instead of using that time to do household chores. Otherwise, I ended up feeling like hired help, knowing that my husband was entertaining clients, more often than not at five-star restaurants.

When my two-month-old son napped for an hour and a half, I would resist the urge to do household chores and instead read, nap, or relax. This "me time" was essential for recharging my energy. When I returned to work, I continued to find ways to give myself "me time." My hour-and-a-half commute became an opportunity to listen to audiobooks unrelated to parenting or work. After long days at the office, I would sometimes drive around the block twice before heading home, giving myself those much-needed extra minutes to regroup before taking on the "mommy shift."

During my thirty-three years of growing a consulting practice, I made it a point to dedicate personal time during flights to watching movies or reading for pleasure. No matter how hectic life became, I knew that setting aside time for myself was essential.

Now, with my children grown and my work schedule less demanding, I still dedicate a minimum of 2 hours daily to myself. Whether it's getting up early or staying up late, I ensure that I have time to recharge—even when our needy Maltese, Mozart, persistently nudges me to go to bed.

Whether you're a new parent, juggling a family and career, or enjoying your later years, what are you doing to carve out time for yourself each day? If you aren't, then start now. It's your first step toward becoming time-affluent.

Your Call to Action

Define one small actionable step that you will take with your own daily to-do list to improve your time affluence—whether it's adding "me time" or something else.

TIME AFFLUENCE TIP FROM A TOP CEO

Jeff Weiner, executive chairman and former CEO of LinkedIn, carves out 2 to 3 hours each day to reflect, think, and see the big picture. Weiner advises that if you do not carve out at least an hour, you are fitting way too much into your schedule.[9]

———————
———————

STEP 5
Create a Customized Time Budget

Time you enjoy wasting is not wasted time.
MARTHE TROLY-CURTIN

In our fast-paced society, it often feels as though there aren't enough hours in a day. The pressures of professional, personal, and social commitments can make time feel like a limited resource that many of us struggle to manage. However, research reveals that the issue is not necessarily about needing *more* time; often, it's about using the time we have more effectively. By setting up a personalized time budget, you can learn to prioritize your most essential tasks, gain control over your schedule, and avoid the common pitfalls of time wasting. This step explores the impact of wasted time, examines everyday time-wasting habits, and provides tools for creating daily and time-blocked budgets that can help you become genuinely time-affluent.

The Reality of Wasted Time: How Much Time Do We Lose?

When we think of budgeting, finances usually come to mind. Our most valuable nonrenewable resource—time—deserves careful budgeting too. Studies show that many of us lose hours daily to unproductive habits, social media, and distractions.

Research conducted by RescueTime,[10] a popular time-tracking app, found that the average worker spends only about 2 hours and 48 minutes of the workday on productive tasks. In an 8-hour workday, nearly 5 hours are lost to distractions or activities that aren't moving us toward our goals.

The biggest workplace distraction is your phone, followed by overly chatty coworkers. Namely, research conducted by Workamajig shows that 90 percent of people believe their cell phone is their largest distractor. In addition, 50 percent of workers admit that their noisy colleagues create the biggest focus issue. Other common distractions at work include:

- The internet: 30%
- Excessive office noise: 25%
- Office gossip: 17%
- Notifications and social media: 15%
- Meetings and emails: 10%
- Boredom: 10%
- Personal problems: 9%
- Workplace changes: 7%
- Snack breaks: 5%[11]

Even outside of work, time-wasting tendencies continue to eat away at our personal lives. Nielsen's *Total Audience Report*, for example, shows that American adults spend over 11 hours per day interacting with media—watching TV, browsing the internet, or scrolling through social media.[12] Much of this time isn't just casual entertainment; it's often unplanned and habitual, leaving us with less time for relationships, hobbies, and self-care.

Common Time Wasters and How They Slip into Our Day

Let's take a closer look at some of the most common time wasters. Many of these activities are so ingrained in our routines that we may not even recognize them as significant drains on our time.

Social Media and Digital Distractions. Social media apps are designed to keep us engaged, drawing us into endless scrolling. According to the *Digital 2021* report by We Are Social, people worldwide spend an average of 2 hours and 24 minutes daily on social media alone.[13] Notifications from smartphones and devices further interrupt focus, leading to micro-distractions that break concentration and require additional time to refocus.

Email and Messaging Apps. Email is a necessary communication tool, yet many of us spend far too much time checking, sorting, and responding to messages. Studies show that professionals spend about 28 percent of the workday managing emails—roughly 2.6 hours per day.[14] Email overload has become such a widespread issue that researchers have coined the term *email fatigue*.

Multitasking. Multitasking is often mistaken for increased productivity, but research shows it is one of the most unproductive habits. A study by the American Psychological Association found that shifting between tasks can cost us up to 40 percent of our productive time.[15] By focusing on one task at a time, we accomplish more in less time.

Overthinking and Procrastination. Overthinking is about indecision and fear, which keeps people stuck in the planning stage, at times causing near paralysis. Procrastination, on the other hand, is about avoidance and delay, often with an awareness that the task still needs to be completed. Both overthinking and procrastination can significantly reduce productivity, leaving people scrambling to finish tasks at the last minute, often with lower-quality outcomes.

Unplanned Meetings and Calls. Workplace meetings are an essential aspect of collaboration, but too often they are unnecessary or overly lengthy. According to a study by Atlassian, the average employee attends 62 meetings a month, with half considered unproductive.[16]

The Solution: Creating a Daily Time Budget

A daily time budget functions similarly to a financial budget. By tracking how we spend our time and setting limits on specific activities, we can maximize productivity while carving out time for the things that truly matter. The idea is not to pack every minute with activity, but to intentionally plan out blocks of time to focus on what's most important to you.

Step 1: Identify priorities and nonnegotiables. Start by listing your high-priority tasks for both personal and professional areas of your life. These might include work responsibilities, family time, exercise, meal preparation, and self-care. Make sure to include nonnegotiables like sleep, meals, and short breaks.

Step 2: Estimate time needs. Estimate how long each of these activities typically takes. Be realistic, and consider adding a small buffer for unexpected events. You don't want to make your budget so rigid that it causes stress.

Step 3: Allocate time and track it. Assign specific times for each activity and try to stick to this schedule for at least one week. You might notice some areas where you need to adjust. The goal is to create a balanced routine that provides time for both work and relaxation.

Personal Story: How I Learned to Budget My Own Time

I used to be overwhelmed by my to-do list. As a business owner, I constantly felt that there weren't enough hours in the day to balance client work, administrative tasks, family time, and self-care. I'd often get to the end of the day feeling like I hadn't accomplished enough, had neglected myself, or both.

The turning point came one morning when I realized that my time felt like a series of random tasks strung together with little intentionality. I started using a time-budgeting method that allowed me to focus on what mattered most—whether it was scheduling uninterrupted work hours or carving out time for a daily walk. I even built in "recharge" blocks, where I would step away from work completely.

The results were dramatic: I felt less stressed, more in control, and more productive. I met deadlines without scrambling, and I finally had time for the things I'd been putting off—like reading and spending time with my family. While time may be finite, with careful planning and a structured budget, it is possible to maximize its impact. I did it and so can you.

By tracking your daily activities, identifying the most common time wasters, and setting a personalized time budget, you'll find yourself more focused, productive, and fulfilled. The goal is not about squeezing more into your day, but about making your time work for you based on your priorities.

Your Call to Action

Don't let another day slip away to unproductive habits! Start creating your personalized time budget today.

Whether you prefer detailed schedules or flexible time blocks, the first step is to track how you currently spend your time. Download a time-tracking app, jot down your daily activities, or simply observe your habits for a week.

If you choose to use a time-tracking app, identify your specific needs and then see how the time-tracking apps you are considering measure up to your requirements. As a starting place, Zapier, a software company that helps create automated workflow, recommends the following:

- Toggl Track for a free time-tracking app
- Memtime for simple automated time tracking
- TrackingTime for visualizing time differently
- Timeular for automated time tracking
- Harvest for ease of use without sacrificing features[17]

Once you've identified your priorities, set aside a few minutes to draft your own time budget. Experiment with different strategies, including the use of the pie chart on the following page, and don't be afraid to adapt as you learn what works best for you.

Your time is precious, so make every minute count. What step will you take today to gain control over your time?

Figure 1 shows what a busy parent's time budget might look like.

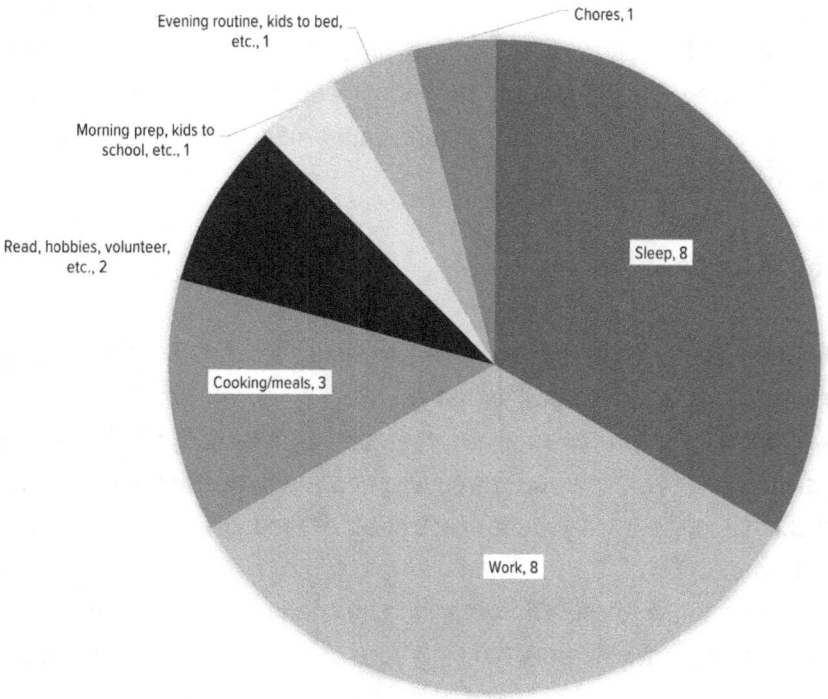

Figure 1: Sample Time Budget – Hours Spent on Daily Activities

You have 24 hours. What does your time budget look like?

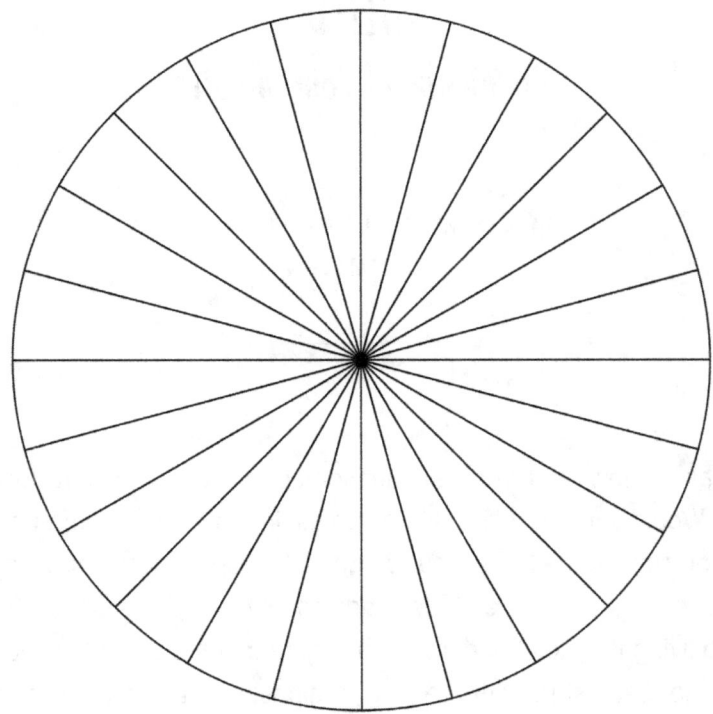

TIME AFFLUENCE TIP FROM A TOP CEO

Ram Krishnan, CEO of PepsiCo Beverages US, says he is "super intentional" about how he uses his time. He organizes every hour of his day in a color-coded pie chart and audits it to ensure he's efficient.[18]

STEP 6
Be Mindful of Your Minutes

Time is what we want most, but what we use worst.
WILLIAM PENN

———————

Think about how often you've heard someone say, "I don't have enough time." Would you describe that person as time-affluent or time-poor?

If you choose the latter, you're right. Like improving other aspects of life, becoming more time-affluent begins with a mindset shift. The first step to living in time abundance is being intentional about how you use your time. Let's start with creating a mindset that helps you be more productive and appreciative of your time wins.

Shift from a Time-Scarcity to Time-Abundance Mindset

Your mindset shapes your life—and your words reflect your mindset. When you say things like "There aren't enough hours in the day" or "I just don't have enough time," you develop a sense of time scarcity. As a result, you're more likely to feel overwhelmed—chasing deadlines instead of creating them, rushing through tasks, and reacting to life rather than controlling how you spend your 24 hours.

But you can change that mindset by reframing how you approach time. Instead of thinking *I don't have enough time*, ask yourself: How can I use my time for what truly matters? This shift empowers you to take control and adopt a more positive can-do attitude toward time. By shifting your mindset from scarcity to abundance, you'll start seeing time as an opportunity to enhance your life rather than as a limitation.

Develop a Quality-over-Quantity Mindset

When thinking of quality over quantity, many consider material possessions. But as we grow, we also begin to place higher value on quality in friendships, intangible things, and even how we use our time. While multitasking sounds appealing—you're getting more done in less time, right?—rushing can lead to mistakes that ultimately cost you more time. By focusing on one task at a time, you'll not only get it done faster, but you'll also do it better.

As Erin Rupp explains in her article "Juggling Multiple Tasks," task-switching is like having multiple tabs open on your computer—it distracts and reduces focus.[19] Rupp outlines three costs of multitasking:

- Reduced accuracy and quality
- Increased time on tasks
- Higher stress levels

Instead of spreading yourself too thin, focus on one project at a time. This mindful approach will help you maintain focus and reduce stress. It isn't just more efficient now—it also contributes to a mindset of time abundance in the long run.

Use Mindfulness in Time Management

Mindfulness isn't just for meditation; it's a powerful tool for time management. You're not alone if you're wondering how mindfulness relates to time efficiency. Like many, I didn't initially connect mindfulness with managing time—until I came across Roberto Benzo's thoughts in a Mayo

Clinic article.[20] His insights helped me realize how mindfulness directly impacts how we spend our minutes daily.

Many people operate on autopilot, jumping from one task to the next without considering whether these activities align with their broader goals. However, a mindful approach to time means being fully present and aware of how you're spending your time. Mindful planning—setting clear intentions for how you will spend your time each day—will do two things: reduce your stress and increase your focus.

Here are three ways to put mindfulness into practice:

- Pause before starting each project and ask yourself: Is this the best use of my time right now?
- Minimize distractions in your workspace by reducing notifications and silencing your phone.
- At the end of each day, review how you spent your time and make adjustments to better align with your goals.

By practicing mindfulness, you'll slow down, focus better, and likely be more productive with less stress.

Your Call to Action

Now it's time to take charge of your day. Block off 10 minutes to plan tomorrow with intention, and set your most important task as the priority. Take control of your minutes; you'll find more time than you thought possible.

TIME AFFLUENCE TIP FROM A TOP CEO

In her book Having It All, *Helen Gurley Brown, known for her determination to minimize idle time, shared one of her famous strategies. When walking in the city, instead of stopping at red lights, she would alter her route, crossing the street in whichever direction the pedestrian signal allowed her to move forward.*[21] *She explained that this approach not only kept her physically active but also aligned with her philosophy of using every moment productively—a testament to her innovative, time-conscious mindset.*

STEP 7
Be Respectful of Others' Time

Everyone should be respected as an individual,
but no one idolized.
ALBERT EINSTEIN

———————
—————

Gifts come in many shapes and sizes, but one of the most valuable gifts you can give is lighter than a feather: the gift of time. Respecting others' time demonstrates that you value their schedules, commitments, and boundaries. I am deeply passionate about punctuality. For me, being prompt isn't just a habit—it's a sign of respect. I also expect others to honor their time commitments, as doing so reflects mutual consideration.

Since patience is not my strongest virtue when I am kept waiting, when I need to make an appointment with a healthcare provider or similar professional, I minimize my stress by scheduling myself for their first appointment of the day whenever possible. Even if it means waiting a month or longer for availability, I prefer this approach over enduring the potential delays that come with a later time slot. After all, once their appointments get off schedule, the delay tends to build throughout the day. My strategy usually avoids that issue.

Are You an Early Bird?

Marissa Higgins would call me an early bird. In her *Bustle* article "Here's Why You're Always Early," she describes early birds as reliable individuals who prioritize their commitments and avoid sliding in at the last second—or worse, arriving late. I'd like to think that my habit of being early reflects responsibility, respect, and conscientiousness.

If you're an early bird, congratulations! Higgins suggests five potential reasons people arrive early:

1. Punctuality was drilled into you during childhood. If you learned to value punctuality as a child and practice it consistently, more power to you! I received this advice often during my youth, but it didn't resonate until much later—three decades later, to be exact. When I finally embraced being early, I discovered the sense of control and calm it brings. To this day, I follow one simple rule to be prompt: Write down the time you need to *leave* rather than the time you need to *arrive*.

2. You may have anxiety. Higgins notes that early arrivers may experience anxiety about running late or fear unforeseen circumstances.

3. You respect others' time. This is the most straightforward reason: Valuing others' time reflects thoughtfulness. We all have limited waking hours; why waste someone else's by being inconsiderate?

4. You assume the worst. Some people plan ahead, expecting delays such as traffic jams or accidents. The worst-case scenario? You'll arrive early—and that's a good thing.

5. You're a natural leader. Setting an example of punctuality shows respect for others and sets expectations for those around you.[22]

Arriving early is a time affluence habit that reflects discipline, consideration, and self-awareness. And if you're still working on it, a small shift—like planning your departure time instead of your arrival time—can make all the difference.

What If Others Keep You Waiting?

People who run late often don't realize they're breaking a verbal commitment. As Susan Krauss Whitbourne, PhD, explains in her *Psychology Today* article "Why It's Such a Bad Idea to Keep Someone Waiting," trust can erode when someone fails to honor a time commitment. Whitbourne also points out that impressions are formed not only by appearance but by behavior—like punctuality.[23]

I'll admit that for the first thirty-four years of my life, I struggled with tardiness. However, after years of practicing punctuality, my tolerance for being kept waiting has vanished. In fact, my annoyance with waiting has occasionally led me to end relationships altogether.

This once occurred at a doctor's office. I had scheduled the first appointment of the day with a physician's assistant (PA) and arrived 10 minutes early to complete the needed paperwork. As I waited, the doctor—who usually saw me on alternate visits—arrived at the office. After 15 minutes, the receptionist informed me that the PA was stuck in traffic and wouldn't arrive for another 30 minutes.

I requested that the doctor, who was available but not seeing patients that day, make an exception and see me. When my request was denied, I politely stated that I would leave if no accommodation could be made. Despite my explanation, the doctor remained unwilling to step in, so I left and never returned to that practice.

It took three months to find a new specialist; however, I have no regrets. That day made it clear how much I value mutual respect—and how time is one of the most telling ways it's shown. Even a quick acknowledgment from the doctor would have gone a long way. Instead, I overheard her laughing and chatting with colleagues about their evening plans. The conversation made it abundantly clear that my time and my presence were not a priority. It left me wondering: Is patient relations an elective in med school?

Whether it's for a doctor, a team meeting, or a coffee date, we all have different thresholds for how much waiting we're willing to accept. Understanding your own limits—and choosing how to respond when they are tested—can help you maintain your standards without losing your cool.

Here are a few respectful ways to handle being kept waiting, especially in healthcare settings, where delays are common:

- **Tolerate the wait.** Accept the delay, understanding that it is sometimes unavoidable. (Emergencies really do occur.)
- **Ask for updates.** A polite inquiry can often clarify how long the delay might last.
- **Reschedule.** If your schedule is tight, ask to move the appointment to a more convenient time.
- **Find a new provider.** If tardiness becomes a pattern, it may be worth researching professionals who value punctuality as much as you do.

There's no universally "right" answer—only the one that aligns with your priorities and values.

Your Call to Action

George Schaefer, former CEO of Fifth Third Bancorp, instilled in his team the following mantra: "When you are five minutes early, you are ten minutes late." To develop a habit of planning ahead and arriving on time consistently, for the next week, record the time you need to leave for each appointment instead of the time you need to arrive. Build in a 10- to 15-minute buffer for unforeseen delays, such as traffic or parking. Track how often you arrive early, on time, or late.

TIME AFFLUENCE TIP FROM A TOP CEO

Andy Bailey, founder of Petra, a business coaching firm, says, "I strive to be on time for every appointment, every day, without exception. This may seem like a no-brainer in the business world, but you would be surprised how many people still don't make it a priority. It's mind-boggling. If a leader is consistently late, it tells others that he or she is unreliable or has no respect for the individuals he or she works with. If he or she is on time, the opposite is true."[24]

PART 3

Plan and Prioritize for Daily Success

STEP 8
Create a Daily Routine

The secret of your success is found in your daily agenda.
JOHN C. MAXWELL

Many of us naturally gravitate toward daily routines. As a kinesthetic learner, I once found the idea of structure confining and rather dull. However, I eventually realized that my aversion wasn't to the routine itself, but to the must-do tasks I had integrated into my daily life. Whatever your relationship with routines, I promise this section will enhance your time affluence.

Three Compelling Advantages of Having a Daily Routine

Even though I buck daily schedules, I have to admit that there are advantages to having one. Below are three:

1. Routine reduces stress and anxiety. Knowing what to expect each day gives your brain a break from constant decision-making. It creates a sense of control and calm, especially during chaotic times.

2. Routine boosts productivity and focus. Routines help you prioritize what matters most. By automating small tasks (like when you eat, work out, or check emails), you free up mental energy for creative and important work.

3. Routine strengthens healthy habits. Doing something consistently—like waking up early, exercising, or reading—makes it second nature. A routine makes it easier to stick to good habits and harder to fall into unproductive ones.

I hope you will recognize, as I did, that a well-crafted routine isn't about restriction. On the contrary, it's about freedom! When your day has structure, your mind has space to focus, your body learns to thrive, and your goals become more achievable.

The Downsides of Routines

While routines can be beneficial, they also have their drawbacks. For some, like my family and pets, daily routines feel comforting. However, I often find them confining. Here are some potential disadvantages:

1. Stifling creativity. Routines can sometimes hamper creativity rather than nurture it.

2. Limiting experiences. Routines may create a sense of limitation in your life, making it feel monotonous.

3. Draining energy. Engaging in scheduled tasks can feel rote and sap your energy, leading to disengagement.

4. Inducing boredom. Simply, a repetitive routine can become boring.

If you find your routine limiting, it may be time to mix things up.

Strategies for a Dynamic Routine

If you want to keep your routine feeling fresh and energizing instead of boring or too straightlaced, here are a few things that work for me:

1. Stay flexible. Instead of locking yourself into rigid time blocks, try giving yourself windows of time for tasks. That way, you can adjust based on how you're feeling or what your energy is like that day.

2. Switch things up. Add a little variety now and then—maybe a new workout, a different route to work, or just changing the order in which you do things. Small changes can bring a surprising spark!

3. Set short-term goals. Short-term goals help keep things interesting and give you something new to aim for. The best part is they are easy to tweak if life throws you a curveball.

4. Check in with yourself. Every so often, ask yourself: Is this routine still working for me? Is it energizing me, or am I dreading it? This type of check-in is essential for keeping things from going stale.

5. Build in downtime. Whatever you do, avoid skipping breaks—whether it's a quick walk, petting your pooch, or doing nada for a bit! Breaks reenergize you and keep your mind clear.

A dynamic routine doesn't have to be flawless; it simply has to feel like you! When you keep your routine flexible, light, and in tune with your energy, your days will flow more naturally. It's not about sticking to a strict plan; it's more about creating a rhythm that feels good and lasts.

Your Call to Action

Are you ready to reclaim your time and energy? Start by designing a daily routine that works *for* you, not *against* you. Structure doesn't have to be stifling; it can be the roadmap that propels you toward your goals while preserving the flexibility you need for creativity and joy.

Here's your next step:

1. **Reflect:** What tasks or habits currently dominate your day? Do they energize or drain you?
2. **Refine:** Start small—add just one new habit to boost your productivity or happiness.
3. **Adapt:** Make your routine dynamic by building in breaks, setting short-term goals, and staying flexible.

Don't wait for the perfect moment. *Now* is the time to create a routine that brings you closer to success while embracing the freedom to thrive.

TIME AFFLUENCE TIP FROM A TOP CEO

Oprah Winfrey is a strong advocate for daily routines because she sees them not as rigid schedules, but as grounding tools—ways to align your actions with your values, create intentionality in your day, and protect your mental and emotional well-being. Oprah emphasizes the importance of a daily routine as a means to manage energy and foster gratitude. She believes that structured daily practices can lead to a more centered and fulfilling life. [25]

STEP 9
Plan Your Day the Night Before

The world makes way for the man who knows where he is going.
RALPH WALDO EMERSON

———————

Did you ever wake up and feel overwhelmed as you tried to figure out what to accomplish that day? There's a good chance you could have minimized that stress by doing one simple thing: planning your day the night before!

That's right—the mere act of jotting down what you intend to accomplish the following day lightens your mental load and helps you jump-start the next 24 hours.

If you doubt that planning your day the night before will work to your benefit, let me tell you about Pamela and Nikki. These professionals have three things in common:

- They each have families to support.
- They each have high-pressure jobs.
- They each work hard—though one works smart, while the other just works hard.

The difference between them? Pamela wraps up each day by mapping out what she wants to accomplish the following day. Nikki, on the other hand, waits until the beginning of each day to figure out which ongoing projects need to be finished and which new projects need to be started.

By mapping out her day at the end of the prior workday, Pamela's advance planning allows her to begin her day with clarity and purpose. She experiences less mental drain and enjoys greater focus as she proactively approaches her goals. As a result, Pamela is consistent in accomplishing tasks and staying on track with her priorities. Nikki, by contrast, feels less in control of her day. Starting her day by planning often leads to decision fatigue, which distracts her from the tasks requiring her attention.

Pamela's proactive planning allows her to direct her energy toward the day's most critical projects, reducing her stress and mental load. Nikki, while equally busy, experiences higher stress levels due to her reactive approach. This lack of structure sometimes leaves her feeling overwhelmed and unproductive.

Which planning style describes you? Are you more like Pamela, whose intentional approach helps her stay productive, or Nikki, whose reactive habits sometimes hinder her progress?

Srinivas Rao, in a Medium article on productivity, offered this planning advice: "If you give yourself a basic framework for your days, you'll be much more likely to plan your days with helpful work that adds value to your life. . . . The first hour of the day is one of the most critical. It sets the tone for what the rest of your day will be like."[26]

Four Strategies for Planning Your Day

To avoid feeling behind each morning, consider the following strategies for planning your day:

1. Start your day early. Even setting your alarm 10 or 20 minutes earlier can shift the tone of your morning. It gives you those extra minutes before the day officially begins.

2. Write it down. Jot down your goals on a sticky note or type them into your phone. The most important thing is to get them out of your head. I can tell you firsthand it will help your mind feel clearer and more grounded.

3. Prioritize your health. Schedule time in your day for a power walk, meals, and a snack or two. When you take care of yourself, the rest of your life is bound to flow better.

4. Stay focused. Check that your to-dos reflect what matters to you.

The more intentionally you plan your day, even by jotting down small tasks, the more in control you will feel. Whether it's on your phone or on paper, having a clear plan helps you to do things with a purpose.

Your Call to Action

Spend 5 to 10 minutes this evening planning for tomorrow. First, list three tasks you completed today that you are proud of. Then, write down your top three priorities for tomorrow; be sure to include one self-care activity, such as exercise, reading, or a meal break. You'll be one step closer to becoming time-affluent.

TIME AFFLUENCE TIP FROM A TOP CEO

At the end of each day, Kevin O'Leary, entrepreneur and Shark Tank *star, plans the next day by writing down the three most important tasks to accomplish. Those three items, whether work or personal, are the first tasks he works on. This helps him spend his time efficiently and focus on what matters.*[27]

STEP 10
Integrate Habit Stacking into Your Life

We are what we repeatedly do.
WILL DURANT

———————

In a world filled with distractions, demands, and decisions, managing time effectively is no longer a luxury—it's a necessity. Whether you're striving for personal growth, greater productivity at work, or simply a more balanced lifestyle, the key lies in optimizing how you use your time. One of the most powerful yet often overlooked strategies to improve time efficiency is habit stacking. Habit stacking, popularized by author James Clear in his book *Atomic Habits*, is the process of linking a new habit to an existing one. Rather than trying to remember to add new tasks into your already full schedule, habit stacking makes use of the cues and rhythms already embedded in your daily life.

Let's explore how this simple strategy works, why it's effective, and how to apply it across different areas of your life.

How Does Habit Stacking Work?

Habit stacking works by leveraging something you're already doing. Instead of forcing your brain to carve out time, motivation, and energy for a new behavior, you anchor it to a habit that's already second nature.

Think of brushing your teeth every morning. It's automatic. What if, immediately after brushing your teeth, you drank a glass of water? Or practiced 2 minutes of gratitude? Over time, your brain would begin to associate the two tasks.

Habit stacking works because it follows the *cue-routine-reward* model of habit formation. When you stack habits, the first habit acts as a natural cue for the next behavior. With repetition, your brain links the two, making the new habit easier to remember and more likely to stick.

Habit stacking also reduces decision fatigue. When you no longer have to decide when or how to perform a habit, you save mental energy—making it easier to stick to the new habit and freeing you up to be more productive elsewhere.

Five Ways That Habit Stacking Can Boost Your Efficiency

Habit stacking offers a low-effort, high-impact method for building new habits without overhauling your entire routine. It boosts your efficiency because it:

1. Minimizes resistance. Attaching new tasks to established habits makes them feel easier and less overwhelming, reducing the tendency to procrastinate.

2. Reduces mental clutter. You don't need to remember to do a new task—it becomes a natural extension of something you already do, freeing up brain space.

3. Saves time with micro-actions. Instead of setting aside large blocks of time, you can make consistent progress with 2- to 5-minute actions slipped into your routine.

4. Creates compound growth. Small habits practiced daily lead to meaningful long-term results, building momentum without requiring major effort.

5. Increases routine stability. Habit stacking brings structure and rhythm to your day, helping you stay grounded and consistent—even during busy or unpredictable periods.

When you align new habits with existing ones, you reduce friction, save mental energy, and create powerful momentum toward your goals.

Seven Areas in Your Life to Integrate Habit Stacking

Habit stacking isn't limited to one part of your routine—it can be a game-changer across all areas of life. Here are seven powerful areas to consider:

1. Health and fitness. Stack habits like drinking water, taking vitamins, and stretching with meals, bathroom routines, or workouts. For example:

- After brushing your teeth, do 10 squats.
- After finishing your morning coffee, prep your lunch.

2. Productivity. Enhance focus and workflow by stacking habits that prepare you mentally and physically for work:

- After sitting down at your desk, review your to-do list.
- After completing a Zoom call, take three deep breaths to reset.

3. Personal development. Grow mentally and emotionally with micro-practices:

- After waking up, say one affirmation.
- After lunch, read one page of a self-development book.

4. Finances. Build money-smart habits into your weekly rhythm:

- After Sunday breakfast, check your bank balances.
- After paying a bill, log it in your expense tracker.

5. Relationships. Be intentional about connecting with others:

- After dinner, send a kind message to a friend.
- After your workday ends, spend 5 distraction-free minutes with a loved one.

6. Spirituality or mindfulness. Add mindful practices to still moments:

- After waking up, do a 1-minute meditation.
- After parking your car, say a gratitude prayer.

7. Home and organization. Improve your environment through tiny, stacked habits:

- After taking off your shoes, tidy one small item.
- After finishing your evening snack, wipe the counter.

When you approach your life with habit stacking in mind, everyday routines become opportunities for growth, connection, and intentional living—one small step at a time.

Your Call to Action

Habit stacking is not a massive overhaul of your life. It's the art of subtle, consistent shifts that amplify your time, focus, and momentum. Whether you're trying to drink more water, improve your finances, or read more books, stacking those desires onto what you're already doing transforms intention into action.

Start small. Pick one existing habit and attach one new habit to it. Practice it for a week. When it becomes second nature, build on to it. Recognize that habit stacking isn't about doing more things—it's about doing the right things automatically.

TIME AFFLUENCE TIP FROM A TOP CEO

Jack Dorsey, co-founder of Twitter (now X) and Square (now Block), is known for his highly structured daily routine, in which he stacks multiple healthy habits together to create consistency and focus. From a 2019 interview: "I wake up, meditate, do a 7-minute workout, make coffee, and then journal—all before checking my phone or email. That sequence keeps me grounded."[28] This is a textbook example of habit stacking: tying new habits (journaling and meditation) to an existing morning routine (waking up and making coffee) so they happen automatically and with less mental resistance.

STEP 11
Create a Daily To-Do List

Plans are useless, but planning is everything.
DWIGHT EISENHOWER

Let me be candid: I hate structure, including making lists. What I do love, however, is getting things done. If you are a list maker like my daughter, creating a daily to-do list may be second nature to you. There's a good chance you've been employing this time management strategy for years. If this time affluence technique is not yet your style, seize the moment! Rather than having umpteen tasks floating around in your mind, free up your brain power and time by making this daily habit a part of your life.

First, let me explain my daily to-do list. It consists of two parts:
- My must-do list.
- My intend-to-do list.

My must-do list includes the tasks with deadlines that either others have requested or I have imposed. I typically limit that list to three items. My must-do list also includes reading incoming email messages and responding to them by day's end. If the response is going to take longer than 10 minutes, however, I acknowledge the message by giving the sender a promised response time. If the request is not urgent, rather than adding it to my must-do list, I note it on my intend-to-do list with a date promised. BTW: I also add key tasks to my calendar as a gentle nudge to myself.

My intend-to-do list includes tasks that I would like to accomplish that day but that are not urgent. They may include following up with someone who has not responded to a message sent within the past 48 hours or running a few errands after work, such as dropping off shoes to be repaired or ordering more office supplies. If the day gets away from me and these intended items do not get done, they are simply moved to the following day. If you are wondering if I limit myself to the number of times they are moved, the answer is yes! Three times is my max. Then they are moved to that good ol' must-do list.

If you wonder where to keep a daily to-do list, that's totally up to you! I use the Notes section of my phone, but you can jot your list on a legal pad, write it on the palm of your hand, use the to-do function in Outlook, or create a Google Keep list. There are many options, so take your pick!

Benefits of a Daily To-Do List

If you are not yet convinced that a daily to-do list will simplify your life, let me ease your mind. Here are five benefits to documenting your to-dos:

1. It provides a framework for your daily commitments. Just as planning a trip allows you to experience more of what you want, having a roadmap for your day allows you to be more productive.

2. It holds you accountable. If you are like me, you are a person of your word. By documenting the task that you commit to getting done, there is a better chance you will do it.

3. It helps you stay realistic about what you can do in a given period. Rather than having pie-in-the-sky ideas about what you are going to get done, a daily to-do list can give you a reality check. My recommendation: Underpromise to yourself what you are going to do each day, and overdeliver by completing your task with time to spare.

Just imagine how good you will feel when you can shut down your computer and close up shop a few minutes early!

4. It gives you a sense of accomplishment when you cross off the completed task. What better than to check off a finished task? If you use separate pieces of paper to jot down tasks, make a spit ball and pitch that paper—it feels *so* good!

5. It keeps you psyched. I will never forget the first time I created a daily to-do list and completed the tasks on it. It felt so freeing! In fact, rather than feeling a sense of dread about the next day as I had in the past, I looked *forward* to the next day! I bet you will too. A daily to-do list allows you to see your workflow in action.

Your Call to Action

Ready to simplify your life and boost your productivity? Start by creating your own daily to-do list. Free up your mental space, track your commitments, and feel the satisfaction of checking off tasks each day. It's a small change that will lead to big results.

TIME AFFLUENCE TIP FROM A TOP CEO

Rachel Blumenthal, former CEO of Rockets of Awesome, a subscription service for children's clothing, says she scribbles her priorities for the day—three to eight things that must be done—on a single sticky note. "A Post-It is great because it can only fit so many to-dos," Blumenthal says. But Blumenthal doesn't stop there; she also scrawls the most important task on her hand—"in between my thumb and pointer finger." That way, she says, "I look at it all day long and can't miss it."[29]

STEP 12
Have a Running To-Do List

We need to do a better job of putting ourselves
higher on our own "to do" lists.
MICHELLE OBAMA

Now that you have read about the value of having a to-do list, have you created one? If not, what are you waiting for? (Come on, if I forced myself to make one, then so can you!) If so, is it one that you recreate daily or weekly? I have to admit, as much as I bucked the idea, I have found that a to-do list really keeps me focused when my mind is running in many directions. Now, please stay with me, because besides creating your own daily to-do list, I am going to encourage you to create a second kind of list: a *running* to-do list.

What Is a Running To-Do List?

The definition of a running to-do list is simple: It's a list filled with projects that you want to accomplish that *may or may not have an end date*. End of story! The items may be part of something in your professional or personal life—completing a business application, attending a networking event, finding a painter to touch up those nicks on your wall, or having that lithograph framed. You get the picture—those kinds of tasks that you need to do, yet they are incomplete, awaiting input, or lower on your priority list.

That being said, when creating a running to-do list, I highly recommend dividing it into projects with a deadline and low-priority projects that you want to accomplish. While your daily to-do list described in Step 11 helps you focus on what you want and need to accomplish, your running to-do list should be used for capturing items that need to be done but are not as pressing. When the time is right, you can move tasks from your running list onto your daily to-do list.

Since I love examples, let me give you a task that was on my daily to-do list but is now on my running list. I contracted with an author to arrange a virtual book tour. As I was filling out the application, I noticed that his birth date was requested by the organization scheduling the tour. I also noticed that the governing organization was requesting a compatible book club guide for the book the author was showcasing. Since the author and I were located in different cities, seven time zones apart, I was at a standstill. So after filling in the other pertinent pieces of information, I saved the document and added the task of completing the application to my running to-do list.

To ensure that the purpose of a running to-do list is clear, let me ask: How would *you* define it? If you described it as an "in progress" or "lower priority" list, you're spot on!

The Benefits of a Running To-Do List

If projects are so low on your list, you may wonder why you should even document them. Here's the primary reason: You will have those low-priority projects in one place rather than having them floating around in your mind. The result: less stress and more mental space to focus on the projects you have designated as high priorities in your life. Additionally, by putting items with no specific deadline on your running list, they are more likely to stay visible and get done rather than fall by the wayside. (I personally sleep better at night knowing I have things written down.)

Need more benefits? Here are five:

1. Increased productivity. If you love being organized, this type of list is a no-brainer for keeping tasks organized and prioritized. It is assurance that no project details will be forgotten.

2. Reduced stress. I don't know about you, but minimizing stress is a big one for me! A running to-do list is a great tool for offloading tasks to a list, making them easier to manage. By documenting what you want to accomplish long-term, you will lighten your load by having an excuse to remove tasks from your daily to-do list that you *should* do sometime but *can* put off at least for the short-term.

3. Better time management. This type of list helps to manage time more effectively. What I love best is that it keeps me from the last-minute scrambling I used to do before I started keeping a running to-do list.

4. Greater accountability. This type of list will give you a clear record of commitments and progress. It will keep you on track.

5. Better focus. When you are clear about what you want to accomplish, you will minimize distractions by keeping your top priorities visible on your daily to-do list. By keeping top priorities front and center, you will be more intentional about what you accomplish!

A running to-do list has two purposes: Besides giving you peace of mind on paper, it takes a weight off your shoulders—I know it does for me. It gives your lesser priorities someplace to live besides your brain.

The Drawbacks of a Running To-Do List

Okay, if you are convinced about creating a running to-do list, I have one more thing to tell you: There are two sides to every coin! While there are plenty of advantages to having a running to-do list, there are also potential drawbacks to watch out for.

1. A running to-do list can give you a false sense of security. While having a running to-do list is great, avoid letting it give you a false sense of security. I fell into that trap once, but no longer. (After all, first time, victim; second time, volunteer!) My recommendation: If you see that a project on your running to-do list has been there for longer than three to six months, either transfer it to your must-do list and give it a deadline, or delete it from your list all together.

2. It can be a procrastination trap. Don't be fooled into believing that having a task documented guarantees action; some people continuously add to their list without completing items. Be sure that does not describe you! Again, periodically identify which tasks need to move to your daily list or be deleted altogether.

3. It causes you to feel overwhelmed. Having a task documented on your running to-do list may make you feel pressured to do it. While that may sound like a negative, it may also act as a great motivator (as it does for me). It serves as a reminder of your self-imposed commitment to complete it. When you do chisel away at it, you will feel a sense of accomplishment; and if it is important enough to keep on the list, it is also important enough to move to your daily to-do list.

4. It results in lack of prioritization. Without proper structure, urgent and important tasks may get lost among less critical ones—if you allow it, that is. I love the lack of structure of a running to-do list. If it is important enough to be documented on your list, then it means that you want to accomplish it. Rather than listing an exact deadline, give it a completion date within a three- to six-month period.

While I wanted to be realistic, I hope you see that the pros of having a running to-do list outweigh the cons. Certainly, a never-ending list can feel daunting, making it hard to know where to start and leading to stress. However, when used strategically, it can become the tool that has been missing in your productivity arsenal: the K.I.T.A. method! (If this acronym is new to you, it means "kick in the ass"!) While the K.I.T.A.

approach may be the push you need to take action, it may not be a lasting tool to keep you motivated. Until you figure out what your intrinsic motivation is, use this external form of pressure as a quick fix.

Pro Tip: Set Some Rules

When I started using a running to-do list, I was more productive. The best part was that I felt less overwhelmed. Here are the three personalized guidelines that I use to this day to optimize my running to-do list:

1. Be selective. Include only tasks that are actionable, measurable, and can be completed in one sitting. This approach will help you to create achievable goals.

2. Do a daily review. Set aside time each morning to review and, if necessary, update your running to-do list. This practice will allow you to adjust priorities based on new information.

3. Prioritize tasks with time blocking. This is by far my favorite personalized guideline. By blocking out time for specific tasks, it forces me to give the needed attention to projects.

So, there you have it!

Your Call to Action

Ready to reclaim your time and mental clarity? Take your first steps to embrace the power of a running to-do list. Transfer tasks that are not priorities but that you'd still like to accomplish from your daily to-do list to your running to-do list. Then decide on some rules for your running list. Test out your process for a month to see how it impacts your productivity and mindset.

TIME AFFLUENCE TIP FROM A TOP CEO

In a 2024 Inc. *article, Steve Taplin, CEO and co-founder of Sonatafy Technology, shares that he primarily uses Google Tasks for his to-do list since it can sync with other Google tools he uses, such as Workspace and Calendar. "That really helps me," he says. "It's not uncommon for me to have over 100 to-do items per day on different topics." The combination of tools allows him to "truly prioritize for the day, for the week, for the month."*[30]

PART 4

Practice Effective Time Management Strategies

STEP 13
Eat That Frog!

If it's your job to eat a frog, it's best to do it
first thing in the morning.
MARK TWAIN

Yes, you read that right: Eat that frog! If you haven't heard this saying before, don't worry—neither had I until recently. Let me give you a little background.

Brian Tracy popularized this phrase in the productivity world through his book *Eat That Frog!: 21 Great Ways to Stop Procrastinating and Get More Done in Less Time*. In Tracy's framework, your "frog" is the most challenging task on your list—the one you're most likely to delay but that would yield the greatest positive impact if completed.

The idea is simple: By finishing this dreaded, difficult, or unpleasant task at the start of your day, you set yourself up for a sense of accomplishment—and the rest of the day feels much more manageable.

How to Identify Your Frog

Finding your frog is easier than you might think. One method is to use what is known as the Eisenhower Matrix. President Dwight D. Eisenhower is quoted as saying, "What is important is seldom urgent, and what is urgent is seldom important." Ain't that the truth! Whether he used this actual productivity tool might be debatable, but the concept of prioritizing tasks based on their urgency and importance is a good one.

Figure 1 shows an Eisenhower Matrix, a 2×2 matrix built on axes of important versus urgent.

	Urgent	Not Urgent
Important	**1. What you MUST do** Tasks with looming deadlines; addressing issues that could lead to major consequences if neglected, e.g., submitting taxes	**2. What you SHOULD do** Skill development and personal growth; relationship-building activities, e.g., networking, mentorship; regular marketing, e.g., writing regular business blog posts
Not Important	**3. What you can DELEGATE** Routine administrative tasks; low-impact tasks that don't require your expertise, e.g., routine social media posts	**4. What you can DELETE** Unnecessary meetings or calls; time-wasting activities, e.g., scrolling social media

Figure 2: Eisenhower Matrix

As you can see, there are four quadrants:

1. What you MUST do. These are tasks with firm deadlines or promises you've made—things that absolutely must get done. Example: Submitting your tax return by month's end. Failing to meet this deadline could lead to penalties, so it's crucial to finish on time.

2. What you SHOULD do. These tasks are important but not urgent. While they would benefit you in the long run, they don't demand immediate attention. Example: Writing a blog post for your company's website.

3. What you can DELEGATE. If you have team members who can take on tasks, delegate them! If not, create templates for future use. Example: Assign routine social media posts to a junior team member.

4. What can be DELETED. Sometimes, tasks that seemed necessary end up being irrelevant. Reevaluate your to-do list regularly. Example: Planning an elaborate office party for a minor holiday.

Your frogs most likely live in quadrants 1 (must do) and 2 (should do).

The Pros of "Eating That Frog"

If you are like most people, some days working on your hardest task first sounds empowering. Other days, it may feel like complete dread! Brian Tracy is a strong believer that "eating that frog" has some real upsides. Below are the pros:

1. It enhances task efficiency. Once you've tackled the hardest task, everything else feels manageable. Scenario: Completing an extensive project report makes organizing your calendar feel like a breeze.

2. You overcome procrastination. Conquering a tough task first builds momentum for smaller ones. Scenario: After making a difficult call to a client, responding to emails feels effortless.

3. It improves work-life balance. Finishing the toughest task frees up energy for other activities. Scenario: Completing preparation for a big presentation lets you focus on smaller tasks distraction-free.

While "eating that frog" provides a clear advantage in boosting productivity and focus, let me tell you: Not every day will be free of distractions. What you can do to stay focused, however, is to prioritize the most difficult task first. By doing so, you will set yourself up for greater success and may be able to tackle the rest of your daily responsibilities with greater ease. The bottom line is that "eating that frog" will help you to create a mindset of discipline.

The Cons of "Eating That Frog"

Now that you know the benefits of "eating that frog," recognize that it also has its drawbacks—especially if you are not a morning person!

1. It can add mental stress. "Eating that frog" can cause mental strain and potential burnout when you constantly prioritize your most challenging tasks first.

2. It can make mornings difficult. Forcing yourself to work on your most difficult task can increase anxiety and apprehension about beginning the workday.

3. It may not be motivating. If you are not a morning person, this strategy may feel overwhelming rather than motivating.

While "eating that frog" can be a powerful strategy, it's important to balance it with self-care and flexibility to avoid being overwhelmed. Recognizing when to take a step back or switch priorities can help maintain long-term productivity and well-being.

Your Call to Action

Ready to give this a try? Use the grid on the following page to identify your frog. Then, eat it now (whatever time of day it is)—complete the task! Tomorrow, identify your frog and eat it first. Repeat daily for greater productivity.

	Urgent	Not Urgent
Important	1. What you MUST do	2. What you SHOULD do
Not Important	3. What you can DELEGATE	4. What you can DELETE

TIME AFFLUENCE TIP FROM A TOP CEO

Andrey Fadeev, CEO of GDEV, a European game development holding, says: "I allocate one hour each day during my peak effectiveness period for these frogs. This way, I don't overwhelm my brain as much, and this doesn't make me unhappy. If you eat one frog a day, you likely [will] be pleasantly surprised at how your life changes in a year."[31]

STEP 14
Touch It Once!

Using the "touch it once" rule for tasks saves time and brain space.
NICOLE BANDES, *COACH'S COPILOT* PODCASTER

———————

If you have not employed the "touch it once" principle—sometimes abbreviated TIO—I hope this step will convince you to do so. In down-to-earth terms, "touch it once" simply means dealing with a task immediately rather than setting it aside and returning to it later.

According to entrepreneur and blogger Chris Ball, the average businessperson wastes over a month each year by revising and rereading information, which Ball labels as a cycle of inefficiency that the "touch it once" principle breaks.

To practice this time-efficient strategy, Ball recommends that you employ these three strategic actions:

1. Immediate organization. Both digital and physical files should be organized and labeled clearly to make retrieval quick.

2. Scheduled email checks. Specific times during the day should be designated to review messages.

3. Decisive task management. This means that tasks are handled immediately or delegated promptly.[32]

Quiz: Do You "Touch It Once"?

If you are unsure how well you employ the "touch it once" principle, take the following quiz. It will allow you to see whether your habits help lead to time affluence.

DIRECTIONS

Circle the letter that best reflects your typical behavior.

1. Morning Coffee Routine
   A. Do you pour your coffee, add cream, and put the carton back in the fridge before your first sip?
   B. Or do you leave the cream out and put it back later?

2. Towel Etiquette
   A. After a shower, do you hang up your towel right away?
   B. Or do you drop it on the floor and deal with it later?

3. Text Message Response
   A. Do you respond to texts that take a minute or less right away?
   B. Or do you read them and respond later?

4. Clothes Management
   A. Do you hang up your work clothes or put them in the hamper after changing?
   B. Or do you leave them on a chair or the floor to deal with later?

5. Grocery Unpacking
   A. Do you put groceries away directly from the bags?
   B. Or do you leave them on the counter and organize them later?

HOW DID YOU SCORE?

Remember, the "touch it once" rule is about handling tasks immediately rather than revisiting them later. This simple habit can boost your time affluence by reducing repetitive actions and preventing unfinished tasks from piling up. For our quiz, all of the A options follow the TIO rule:

1. Coffee: Putting the cream back in the fridge right away means one less thing to think about later, giving you more time to enjoy your beverage.

2. Towel: Hanging your towel up immediately keeps your space tidy and your mind clear, avoiding that "I'll do it later" feeling.

3. Texts: Replying to a quick text right away frees up mental space, so you don't have to remember to do it later.

4. Clothes: Taking care of your work clothes as soon as you change prevents clutter from piling up, keeping your living space serene.

5. Groceries: Putting groceries away right after shopping means no clutter and less effort later.

By embracing the "touch it once" approach, you streamline your routines, reduce repetitive tasks, and avoid mental clutter. After all, time management is about managing the little things that over a day, week, or year can rob you of your time. It can be something as small as touching a piece of paper or retrieving an email that may take a mere 5 minutes of your precious time. And taking those 5 minutes of your precious 5 days a week for 50 weeks a year equates to an extra 1,250 minutes annually. I don't know about you, but I'd rather use those extra 21 hours to do as I please by implementing the "touch it once" rule!

Your Call to Action

Which "touch it once" activities could you do better? Start small, focus on consistency, and enjoy the benefits of being more time-affluent.

TIME AFFLUENCE TIP FROM A TOP CEO

The late Tony Hsieh, former CEO of Zappos, would immediately address emails that required quick responses and allocate specific times to handle more complex messages. By doing so, Hsieh minimized the mental load of pending communications and maintained a clear focus on his priorities. This practice reflects the essence of the "touch it once" principle—addressing tasks decisively to prevent them from lingering and consuming unnecessary attention.[33]

STEP 15
The 2-Minute Rule: Do It Now!

A good plan violently executed now
is better than a perfect plan next week.
GEORGE S. PATTON

With 1,440 minutes in a day, the real question is how efficiently you use these 60-second increments. Since this book is titled *The Wannabe Minute Master*, I want to highlight David Allen's "2-minute rule" from his best-selling time management book, *Getting Things Done: The Art of Stress-Free Productivity*.

Allen defines the 2-minute rule simply: If a task takes less than 2 minutes, do it immediately.

When I first came across this rule, I realized I was already practicing it daily without even knowing it. There's a good chance you are too. Why? Because no one enjoys seeing their to-do list grow. Knocking out small, simple tasks as soon as they arise helps prevent the list from becoming overwhelming.

Here are a few ways I applied this rule just this morning:
- I made my bed the moment I got out of it.
- I put clothes in the dryer while passing the laundry room.
- I replied "yes" to my daughter's text about a 7:30 a.m. call.
- I sent a thank-you text to a friend for dinner last night.

- I responded to a meeting confirmation for tomorrow.
- I downloaded an audiobook for my walk to the office.
- I ordered Hint Water from Amazon in three clicks.

These quick wins took less than 2 minutes each and made my morning feel more productive.

When to Use the 2-Minute Rule

Below are lists of common personal and professional tasks. If you find yourself doing any of these regularly, give yourself credit for being a 2-minute taskmaster! If not, ask yourself why you're putting them off.

Personal tasks:

- Responding to a simple email or text
- Filing documents
- Washing dishes immediately after use
- Refilling your water bottle
- Decluttering your space
- Reading a motivational quote
- Updating a shopping list
- Rescheduling an appointment

Professional tasks:

- Confirming a meeting
- Forwarding emails
- Updating your calendar as you schedule
- Refilling office supplies
- Organizing documents or saving files
- Proofreading a quick email

I use the 2-minute rule daily, because it feels good to clear out the quick to-dos from my list, but it is also great to apply to get started on a bigger project. If you break your large project into small tasks, doing a few quick ones first can help you gain momentum.[34]

As you try the 2-minute rule, consider whether it works best for you to group a bunch of tasks together in sequence, or to spread them out and address them as they arise. If your goal is to stay focused, handling 2-minute tasks back-to-back can give you a sense of accomplishment and prevent them from piling up. However, doing too many in succession can sap your energy for bigger tasks. And sometimes a 2-minute task is a nice break between bigger projects. Find the balance that works for you.

Is There a Downside to the 2-Minute Rule?

While this 2-minute rule is a great tool, it can have its drawbacks. In an article on MSN, John Rampton warns that overusing it can lead to potential challenges:

1. Overwhelm. It can overwhelm you with too many small tasks. When that happens, prioritize the tasks that are the most urgent.

2. Context switching. Constantly switching between tasks, even small ones, can be counterproductive—to say nothing of being mentally exhausting.

3. Underestimating time. Due to distractions or unexpected complications, 2-minute tasks can sometimes take longer. It's helpful to build in a buffer.[35]

For me, though, the biggest problem with the 2-minute rule is becoming caught up in completing too many small tasks and not paying attention to bigger—more important—tasks. Recall our discussion in Step 13 about important versus urgent tasks. Sometimes when I can't get my project engine revved to delve into a big project on my daily to-do list, I find myself procrastinating by doing a lot of the 2-minute projects that are on my running to-do list. While I *am* getting them out of the way, I also recognize that doing them is sometimes a form of procrastination for the project staring at me with an end-of-day deadline!

Your Call to Action

Now that you understand the power of the 2-minute rule, it's time to put it into practice. Start identifying tasks you can complete quickly, both in your personal and professional life. Don't let your to-do list pile up!

TIME AFFLUENCE TIP FROM A TOP CEO

In a 2017 time management article on Business Insider, *Josh Zerkel, then the director of global community and training at Evernote, said, "If you can do something right now in the moment, without having to close it and then reopen it again later, get it done now."*[36]

STEP 16
Stay Focused

Focus is about saying no.
STEVE JOBS

———————
———————

Now that you've read about the "touch it once" principle and the 2-minute rule, this is a great time to *stay focused*.

Maintaining focus is crucial, because it enhances your productivity by allowing you to complete projects more efficiently. Staying focused also improves the quality of your work and decision-making. Doing one thing at a time also minimizes stress by preventing that overwhelming feeling that comes from juggling multiple tasks simultaneously. Cal Newport, author of *Deep Work: Rules for Focused Success in a Distracted World*, popularized the term *deep work*, meaning uninterrupted work performed on tasks that are cognitively challenging. He contrasts it with the "shallow" work that fills most of our daily schedules. Newport advocates dedicating focused time to these demanding tasks. The ability to concentrate on deep work is an essential quality for producing meaningful results.

Common Distractions and How to Minimize Them

Distractions are the primary culprits behind lost focus. Once you recognize how much time they waste, you'll work harder to minimize them. I certainly did after learning that, according to Gloria Mark, professor and researcher at the University of California, Irvine, "It takes an average of about 25 minutes (23 minutes and 15 seconds, to be exact) to return to the original task after an interruption."[37]

It's clear that distractions sabotage your focus and prevent you from being time-affluent. You probably know what some of your regular distractions are, but let's just mention a few common ones and how to manage them:

Smartphones. Keep them silent and out of sight. This eliminates the temptation to check notifications, messages, and social media alerts.

Noise. Find a quiet space to work or use headphones to block out noise pollution.

People interruptions. Throughout my career, I've discovered two effective solutions for avoiding interruptions:

- **Working during off-hours.** When my family is asleep, I set aside focused work time. For example, I often wake up at 4:30 a.m. or stay up late. (In fact, I'm writing this tip at 1:00 a.m., and I hope not even a mouse is stirring.)
- **Hiding.** On tight deadlines, I pack my laptop and head to a secret location within four blocks of my home. My family doesn't know exactly where it is, but I get more done in 3 hours there than in an entire day surrounded by loving interruptions like "What's for lunch?" or my pup barking for a treat.

Multitasking. Avoid multitasking. Multitasking is the opposite of focus. While it may *seem* efficient, it often takes longer to complete tasks and reduces overall productivity. If your goal is to become time-affluent, multitasking is a losing proposition. However, while monotasking is usually the best strategy, there are situations where multitasking can work in your favor. For example, combining activities that don't require intense focus—such as listening to a podcast while power walking—can be a productive use of time.

Distractions are inevitable, yet they don't have to rule your life. By practicing one or more of the strategies above, you can focus on tasks that matter. The more intentional you are, the more time-affluent you will become, one step at a time.

Your Call to Action

When distractions threaten your ability to stay focused, what steps can you take to minimize them? Commit to making changes that allow you to protect your time and attention.

TIME AFFLUENCE TIP FROM A TOP CEO

Andrew Marsh, CEO of Fifth Column Games, has developed a system to help people work without being interrupted. Employees place a "cone of silence" on their desks—a tangible symbol to others not to disturb them unless it's an emergency.[38]

———

STEP 17
Set Boundaries

Daring to set boundaries is about having the courage to love ourselves, even when we risk disappointing others.
BRENÉ BROWN

———————

When was the last time you were worn out at the end of your workday, yet you still had email messages to return, a proposal to get to your client, and family waiting for you to come home? How much of your day did you give to others when you could have focused on the tasks that were still left undone?

What about when someone asked for your time, and you agreed despite knowing you'd regret it? Or when you said no and felt guilty for not sharing your precious time?

To handle these situations better, establish time boundaries that prioritize what you need for yourself. Then, communicate your availability—or unavailability—clearly and confidently.

Four Advantages of Setting Time Boundaries

Setting boundaries is not a selfish act. It's a form of time management and will enhance your quality of life. Some of the benefits include:

1. Increased productivity. Allocating specific time slots for tasks

85

helps you focus better, reduce procrastination, and complete tasks more efficiently, ensuring that important work gets done within the set time-frame.

2. Reduced stress and burnout. Scheduling defined start and end times for tasks allows you to recharge by building in relaxation time. This balance is crucial for maintaining mental and physical health.

3. Better work-life balance. Time boundaries create space for family, friends, and personal activities. They allow you to focus on your tasks and ensure you have time to relax and enjoy life.

4. Enhanced focus and concentration. Isn't it interesting how you tend to accomplish more when you're short on time—like the week before a vacation? Time boundaries minimize distractions and help you stay focused.

Setting time boundaries can feel challenging, especially when you're pulled in multiple directions. Whether it's an unrealistic project deadline or a family member pressuring you to commit time you simply don't have, establishing clear time boundaries is essential.

Think Before You Agree: Diplomatic Responses

It's natural to feel conflicted when you have to say no to someone you care about, be it a family member, friend, boss, or colleague. Setting time boundaries requires tact and clarity to ensure you maintain relationships while respecting your own priorities.

Oftentimes the words you use can make or break how the receiver hears them. When delivering your response regarding boundaries, keep these guidelines in mind:

- Use "I" statements to take ownership of your time.
- Express gratitude for being asked, even when declining.
- Offer alternatives, when possible, to show willingness to help within your limits.

By clearly communicating the time you can offer, you soften the impact and help prevent others from taking your response personally.

Here are nine common situations and some sample responses you might use—adapt as needed!

1. Family Obligations
- Sample response: "I'd love to help, but my schedule is packed right now. Let's plan for a specific time that works for both of us."
- Why it works: It balances empathy with firm boundaries and offers an alternative.

2. Friends in Need
- Sample response: "I want to support you, but I have some pressing commitments. Can we talk later this week when I can give you my full attention?"
- Why it works: Your message shows you care while setting a timeframe that works for you.

3. Work Requests from Colleagues or Bosses
- Sample response: "I'd be happy to help, but I am currently focused on [specific task]. Would it be okay to address this after [specific time] or delegate it to someone else?"
- Why it works: It communicates priorities and offers solutions without outright refusal.

4. Volunteer Situations
- Sample response: "I really appreciate the opportunity, but I'm unable to commit at this time. Please keep me in mind for future opportunities when my schedule is more open."
- Why it works: Your response declines respectfully while leaving the door open for future participation.

5. Requests from Children
- Sample response: "I can help you with that after I finish [specific task]. Let's set aside time later to work on it together."
- Why it works: It reinforces boundaries while showing support.

6. Favors for Neighbors
- Sample response: "I'd love to help, but I'm tied up today. Could we revisit this later in the week, or would someone else be able to assist?"
- Why it works: Your answer offers an alternative and gently declines immediate involvement.

7. Mentorship or Guidance
- Sample response: "I value helping others, but my time is limited right now. I would be happy to answer specific questions via email or schedule a brief call next week."
- Why it works: It provides structured support within your availability.

8. Charitable Donations of Time
- Sample response: "Your cause is so important, but I'm currently stretched thin. I'd be happy to contribute in another way or recommend someone who might be able to help."
- Why it works: It expresses support without overcommitting.

9. Support for Spouse
- Sample response: "I understand this is important to you. Can we set aside time to discuss it after [specific obligation] so I can give it my full attention?"
- Why it works: It provides for their needs while managing your own schedule.

Setting boundaries means you are prioritizing your own time and energy. With thoughtful, supportive responses, you will be respecting your schedule without ruining your relationships.

Your Call to Action

Whether it's in your personal, professional, or social life, start setting time boundaries today. Think about the areas where you feel the most stretched. Then set clearer limits that will better protect your time and energy. Rather than being guilted into saying yes, remind yourself that saying no is not about rejection; it's about making space for what truly matters. By honoring your time boundaries, you will be committing to what matters most to you. Take the first step now and set a boundary that supports the life you want to lead.

TIME AFFLUENCE TIP FROM A TOP CEO

Warren Buffet, the world's most famous investor, says, "People are going to want your time. It's the only thing you can't buy. I can buy anything I want, basically, but I can't buy time."[39]

STEP 18
Use Meeting Agendas

By failing to prepare you are preparing to fail.
ANONYMOUS

———————

Just as you plan your route before scheduling a flight, taking public transportation, or embarking on a road trip, having a set agenda is essential when organizing a formal meeting. An agenda adds structure to the gathering and makes good use of one of our most valuable commodities: time.

If you've ever attended a meeting that lacked structure, you may have found it to be a frustrating waste of time. (And it doesn't matter whether it was in person or via video.) This frustration could have been avoided with proper organization.

Of all the monthly meetings I attend, there is one I anticipate the most for a simple reason: It is well structured. The chair of that committee is a master of time management. Let me share the process he uses so that you can incorporate it into your upcoming meetings.

Advance agenda. Three to five days before the scheduled meeting, an agenda is sent to each participant. It lists the discussion topics, assigns roles, and defines the time allocated for each segment.

Arrival. On the day of the meeting, each attendee is expected to arrive 10 minutes before the meeting starts. Although this expectation is never stated explicitly, the chair consistently arrives early, teaching by example that actions speak louder than words.

Meal orders. If it's a lunch meeting, orders for beverages and meals are taken before the meeting starts.

Call to order. The chair promptly calls the meeting to order at the scheduled time, regardless of whether all attendees have arrived. This sets a precedent for respecting everyone's time.

Minutes. Participants are asked to review minutes from the previous meeting. A motion to approve them is made and seconded. A designated person takes minutes to document any discussion throughout the meeting.

Agenda topics. The chair follows the agenda, ensuring all participants are engaged.

- If a topic doesn't reach a conclusion, the chair either calls for a vote or suggests continuing the discussion at the next meeting.
- If the meeting runs over time, remaining topics are either discussed quickly, deferred to the next meeting, or addressed in a smaller group with the outcome shared later.

Next meeting. The next meeting date is then confirmed, and the meeting is adjourned.

Sounds easy? It is—when a meeting has a structured agenda!

How to Take Back Time When a Meeting Gets Derailed

Even with a great agenda, meetings can sometimes get off track. Here's how to handle seven common challenges:

1. Off-topic discussions. Gently steer the conversation back to the agenda to maintain focus. For example: "Great point—let's capture that for a follow-up discussion and come back to our agenda for now." "Let's park that thought in the interest of time and revisit it if we have a few minutes at the end."

91

2. Dominating participants. Encourage quieter attendees to share their perspectives to balance the discussion. For example: "Let's hear from some voices we haven't had a chance to hear yet—any thoughts from those who've been quiet?" "That's a helpful point—let's open the floor to others who might see it differently or want to add on."

3. Technical difficulties. Have a backup plan to minimize delays caused by internet issues or other technical problems. For example: "While we sort this out, let's move forward with what we can—thanks for your patience." "Tech happens—let's keep moving with what we have and circle back once we're fully connected."

4. Disputes or conflicts. Address differing opinions diplomatically, aiming for a constructive resolution. For example: "It's great to have passionate input—let's focus on common ground and next steps we can agree on." "It's clear we care about getting this right—how about we focus on actionable solutions from here?"

5. Late arrivals. Avoid backtracking for latecomers; instead, bring them up to speed briefly during a natural pause. For example: "Welcome— I'll catch you up during a quick break so we can keep our momentum going." "Glad you're here—we'll touch base after the meeting so we don't lose our rhythm."

6. Analysis paralysis. Push for decisions rather than endless discussion by setting clear deadlines. For example: "Let's land on a decision by [specific time], and we can always revisit if new info comes up." "We've explored this thoroughly—let's commit to a direction so we can start making progress."

7. Multitasking participants. Remind attendees to stay focused and minimize distractions during the meeting. For example: "Let's all stay present so we can wrap this up efficiently—thanks for your focus." "Let's give this our full attention—this way we can finish sooner and avoid follow-up meetings."

Addressing these issues requires tact and strong facilitation. A clear agenda and established ground rules are crucial for keeping a meeting on track. Besides enhancing efficiency and reducing wasted time, having an agenda and helping people stick to it shows respect for participants' time, leading to more productive outcomes and extra time for personal activities.

Bonus Topic: When You Are the Meeting Attendee

When accepting a meeting invitation, ask the organizer: "What may I do to prepare for the meeting?"

This question not only demonstrates your initiative; it also helps the organizer structure the meeting more effectively by considering your role.

Your Call to Action

Start applying these strategies in your next meeting. Take the lead in organizing with a clear agenda and watch how it transforms the efficiency and effectiveness of your gatherings.

TIME AFFLUENCE TIP FROM A TOP CEO

Satya Nadella, Microsoft's CEO, has three simple tips for running a great meeting: Listen more. Talk less. Be decisive when the time comes to make solid decisions. [40]

PART 5

Maximize Time and Technology

STEP 19
Stop Time-Leaking Conversations

There is no greater harm than that of time wasted.
MICHELANGELO

How often do conversations eat up your day? I don't mean the meaningful chats that build connections or the lighthearted banter that fills your soul. I mean the unscheduled, meandering prattles that siphon away your precious minutes—those "time-leaking" conversations that serve no purpose and leave you wondering, *Why didn't I excuse myself sooner?*

I remember one instance vividly. It was a Monday morning, and I had a packed schedule. As I was grabbing coffee, a colleague cornered me with what started as a quick question. Fifteen minutes later, I realized I was listening to an unsolicited deep dive into their weekend drama. Every attempt to pivot the conversation was met with more detail, and I couldn't find a polite way out. By the time I escaped, I was stressed and behind on my day.

That moment taught me a valuable lesson: It's not rude to protect your time; it's necessary. Time-leaking conversations are a common productivity trap, but with the right strategies, you can handle them gracefully while maintaining positive relationships.

How to Identify Time-Leaking Conversations

Time-leaking conversations follow some common patterns. Watch for these possible leaks:

- **Unstructured chat:** Conversations that meander with no clear purpose or end in sight.
- **TMI overload:** Sharing irrelevant details that derail the topic.
- **Meetings that should be emails:** Time spent discussing topics that could have been handled with a quick message.
- **Casual chatter interruptions:** Informal talks that disrupt your workflow.
- **Monopolized discussions:** When someone dominates the conversation without generating actionable outcomes.

Recognizing these patterns is the first step toward reclaiming your time. By becoming more intentional about how and when you engage with others, you can plug leaks and steer your conversations toward clarity, connection, and purpose.

Three Strategies for Setting Boundaries

By setting clear boundaries, you can head off time-leaking conversations, steer discussions toward purpose, and preserve your time. Here are three strategies for doing so:

1. Preempt the request. Let's say you know a meeting or chatty coworker is on the horizon. Set a clear time boundary up front: "I'm working on a tight schedule today, so I can give you 15 minutes—let's make the most of it." This establishes expectations and helps keep the conversation focused.

2. Drive toward a close. During long conversations, summarize the discussion: "Before we wrap up, let's confirm the next steps." This polite cue redirects the conversation and signals a conclusion.

3. Perfect the art of interruption. If a conversation is spiraling, try subtle cues like shifting your body language or tapping your pen. If that doesn't work, interject tactfully: "That's an interesting point, but let me add something briefly before I forget." Or try: "We are getting tight on time. Can you bottom-line it for me?"

By implementing these strategies, you can effectively manage your time and maintain focus. Setting clear boundaries will not only enhance your productivity; it will also encourage respectful and purposeful interactions.

When Basic Boundaries Aren't Enough

Sometimes, you need to take stronger measures to protect your time. Three possibilities:

1. Have a catchphrase. Keep a polite yet firm line ready, like "I'd love to continue this, but I need to jump back into my project."

2. Use a physical signal. Put on headphones or display a Do Not Disturb sign to indicate focus.

3. Find a hiding place. If distractions persist, relocate to a quiet space where you can work undisturbed.

When basic boundaries fall short, these assertive strategies can help you reclaim your time and focus. By proactively managing your interactions, you reinforce your commitment to productivity and well-being.

Your Call to Action

Your time is one of your most valuable resources—guard it fiercely! This week, identify one time-leaking conversation and test one of the strategies above. Protecting your time doesn't mean being impolite; it means setting boundaries that enable you to focus on what truly matters.

TIME AFFLUENCE TIP FROM A TOP CEO

Jensen Huang, CEO of Nvidia, has an interesting approach to keeping employees from rambling. From the book The Nvidia Way, *author Tae Kim notes: "When an employee starts rambling, Jensen will say 'LUA,' which he pronounces like a single word: Looh-ahh. Bryan Catanzaro, [an] Nvidia executive, explained that LUA is a warning sign that Jensen's patience is growing thin. When he says it, Jensen wants the employee to stop and do three things: Listen to the question. Understand the question. Answer the question.* "[41]

STEP 20
Minimize Wait Time

Spread your wings—today. Why wait?
JONATHAN LOCKWOOD HUIE

———————

According to a 2022 survey by Waitwhile, Americans spend roughly 37 billion hours each year waiting in line.[42] That doesn't even include being kept waiting by a friend, family member, client, work associate, or—worse yet—someone you are paying to render a service, such as a doctor or lawyer whose billable hours are out the wazoo!

I don't know about you, but I see waiting for scheduled appointments and gatherings as a big waste of time. Granted, many people find ways to use that gap time productively (as we'll discuss in Step 21: Leverage Dead Time). However, no matter how you cut it, keeping someone waiting shows a lack of respect for that person.

Before I give you some strategies for minimizing wait time, let me share some fascinating research. In a 2020 article on the Society Pages website, Nick Mathews shares a summary of various research on waiting, including this interesting point:

> A difficult part of waiting is that we often do not know how long we will wait. For example, how long will we wait for a coronavirus vaccine? Research has found the importance of

temporal specificity, meaning the presence or absence of a deadline as an assurance of action. A specific timeframe, telling a person when the waiting will end, gives "some degree of control over the situation, through knowledge" (Rotter, 2016).[43]

And David Maister's article "The Psychology of Waiting Lines," while from 1985, still seems relevant to me. Maister asserts that how long the wait feels may have little correlation to the actual time we wait. He compiled the following list of eight factors that affect our perception of waiting:

1. Occupied time feels shorter than unoccupied time. My perspective: If you were a Scout growing up, you know the motto: "Be prepared." When you are kept waiting, use your time wisely by replying to email messages, listening to your favorite podcasts, or meditating. By occupying yourself during wait time, the time is likely to feel shorter than the time you are actually kept waiting.

2. People want to get started. My perspective: Did you know there is a psychology to being handed a menu in a restaurant when shown to a table? It helps customers become acquainted with what is on the menu and accelerates the order process when the server is ready to take the order. It also keeps guests busy by having something to do.

3. Anxiety makes waits seem longer. My perspective: Often, worrying about a situation is worse than the situation itself. That includes being stuck in traffic while driving to the airport to catch a flight or experiencing meeting delays that impact back-to-back scheduling.

4. Uncertain waits are longer than known, finite waits. My perspective: When waiting to board a delayed flight, it is much less stressful to be told when I will board than it is to be left without updates. Even when I am told by a gate agent the projected flight boarding time, I often call the airline's customer service line to confirm it matches.

5. Unexplained waits are longer than explained waits. My perspective: When a flight is delayed and a gate agent says, "We have no information," it is frustrating. Rather than holding my breath, I do what I can to get the reason by calling the airline.

6. Unfair waits are longer than equitable waits. My perspective: To me, part of a fair wait is that the person who has waited the longest is taken care of first. When that doesn't happen, there's a good chance the early bird will not be a happy camper.

7. The more valuable the service, the longer the customer will wait. My perspective: This statement is true most of the time. While we might tolerate waiting for a doctor to run behind, most people won't wait for a table in a restaurant.

8. Solo waits feel longer than group waits. Waiting alone often feels longer because there is less distraction and there are fewer external stimuli to occupy your mind. When you're alone, you're more likely to focus on the passage of time, amplifying your awareness of each minute ticking by. By contrast, being with others—especially more than one person—offers conversation, shared observations, and just the energy of presence, which shifts your focus outward.

Let me give you two scenarios:

First, imagine you're alone at a restaurant waiting for a table. You check your phone repeatedly, glance at the hostess stand, and start to notice how slowly the minutes seem to pass. Every few moments you wonder, *How long has it been?*

Now imagine you're waiting with two friends. You're chatting about your day, laughing at a shared memory, maybe commenting on the décor or the menu. Suddenly, the host calls your name, and you realize you barely noticed the wait at all. The time felt shorter—not because it was, but because your attention was elsewhere.

Six Tips for Minimizing Wait Time

As we've mentioned a few times, time is your most valuable resource. Below are four strategies for minimizing wait times:

1. Schedule the first appointment of the day. First appointments are less likely to run late or be rescheduled. Having an early appointment will also help you to set the pace for a productive, focused day.

2. Get there early! Arriving 5 to 10 minutes early gives you time to settle in and think clearly. It signals reliability and preparedness and shows respect for others' time—all of which boost your trustworthiness and give you an advantage.

3. Set clear expectations about your time constraints. Let people know how much time you have before a meeting starts. This may encourage a prompt start.

4. Build good relationships. Good relationships grease the wheels of collaboration and communication. They help avoid delays caused by confusion, resistance, or distrust.

Small shifts like arriving early and setting expectations may lead to time efficiency. When you take control of your time, you are sending a message to others that time matters.

Your Call to Action

Don't let delays drain your day. Take charge of your time by identifying where you're waiting—and why. Start by tracking just one recurring delay this week and replace it with something purposeful. Small shifts can lead to big gains in momentum.

TIME AFFLUENCE TIP FROM A TOP CEO

Steve Ballmer, former CEO of Microsoft, creates a budget to manage his time. He has a spreadsheet that his assistants have access to, where time is assigned in his budget to those who need to meet or speak with him. This helps him manage his time and make sure he isn't spending too much time on unnecessary things. [44]

———————

STEP 21
Leverage Dead Time

Lost time is never found again.

BENJAMIN FRANKLIN

How well do you make the most of "dead" time? I'm not talking about your well-deserved time to decompress, but those wasted minutes spent commuting, waiting in lines, or sitting in doctors' offices. These moments, though seemingly minor, add up. For instance, the average American spends 60 minutes commuting daily, which equals about three years over a lifetime.[45] While remote work (much of it instigated by the COVID-19 pandemic) may have reduced commute times for some people, many companies are instating return-to-office mandates, so commutes could reappear as a time management issue for many of them.

And then there is waiting, waiting, waiting... A Timex survey revealed that Americans spend an average of:

- 20 minutes daily waiting for buses or trains
- 32 minutes waiting per doctor visit
- 28 minutes waiting in security lines when traveling
- 21 minutes waiting for a significant other to get ready
- 13 hours annually waiting on hold for customer service[46]

It's time to use those minutes more effectively. Turn "dead" time into "alive" time!

Transforming Dead Time into Alive Time

New York Times bestselling author Robert Greene differentiates between dead time and alive time. He describes dead time as time spent being passive, unengaged, and letting external circumstances dictate your experience—time that is not your own. Alive time, on the other hand, is when you are learning, creating, and progressing in your development or toward your goals—time when you are being the boss of your experience![47]

Sometimes all it takes to turn dead time into alive time is a shift in how you view an experience. A "dead-end job" can turn into a "learning-what-I-don't-like experience." But at a tactical level, there are many ways to transform dead time, including the following:

1. Listen to audiobooks or podcasts. Robin Sharma, in his book *The 5AM Club*, calls commute time "Traffic University," as it is an opportunity to learn and grow.[48]

2. Read or listen to industry news. Subscribe to relevant email newsletters for updates tailored to your interests.

3. Learn a new language. Use apps like Duolingo or Babbel to practice languages during idle moments.

4. Plan your day. Utilize calendar apps to reorganize priorities during unexpected delays.

5. Brainstorm ideas or write. Use downtime creatively as one writer did, drafting an entire novel while commuting.

6. Practice mindfulness or meditation. Even a few moments of mindfulness can enhance well-being.

7. Respond to texts and emails. Use small pockets of time to clear your inbox.

8. Practice gratitude. Reflecting on what you're thankful for can turn idle moments into meaningful ones.

Rather than letting life's in-between moments slip away, use them to your advantage. Whether you are stuck in traffic or waiting in line, turn those minutes into useful time. By doing so, you will see how those small shifts can make for a more productive life.

Your Call to Action

Rather than letting dead time slip away, try implementing one of these strategies each day. Share your successes with others to inspire them to become more time-affluent too!

TIME AFFLUENCE TIP FROM A TOP CEO

David Goldin, CEO and founder of Capify, does his best to make the most of drive time. He says, "While it can be frustrating at times to have a long commute, not to mention often getting stuck in traffic, I find this time very useful for scheduling calls that are uninterrupted. It also allows me to accomplish a lot more for the day when I get into the office, knowing these important conversations have already taken place and I can focus on other matters."[49]

STEP 22
Use Digital Technology to Your Advantage

*Automation does not need to be, we hope, our enemy. . . . I think
machines can make life easier for men, if men do not let the
machines dominate them.*

JOHN F. KENNEDY

———————

Some view technology as a time thief, while others see it as a powerful tool for increasing efficiency. Both groups are right—the key is how you use this twenty-first-century innovation to your benefit.

Technology has surely made life faster and more convenient. Think about it:

- The hour we save by ordering groceries, clothes, and other essentials online.
- The time we save by watching movies at home instead of heading to the theater.
- The time saved by videoconferencing tools—no need to travel by car, plane, or camel!

Yet, even with the time-saving tools we already use, are we truly making the most of them?

Using technology to automate or streamline helps you reduce context-switching, create consistency, and dodge burnout. With fewer manual decisions and more things running on autopilot, you have less brain drain and can save energy for what really counts—like having quality relationships with family, friends, and colleagues.

Let's explore strategies to help you reclaim even more of your precious time. While setting up digital tools does take time (with some taking more time than others, especially if you are not tech-savvy), the time spent up front will reap benefits down the road.

Strategy 1: Automate repetitive tasks.

There are many tools that can perform common, repetitive actions for you via automation. Consider these possibilities.

Email management. Many of us spend a good part of our day on email. Did you know you can:

- Automatically filter and sort incoming emails into folders, apply labels, or mark them "read" based on sender, subject, or keyword?
- Automatically respond to let people know you are away?
- Use templates (canned responses) for standard replies?
- Write an email now and schedule it to be sent later (which is great for time-zone differences)?
- Use a tool like Zapier to save email attachments to a designated location automatically?

Exploring these options and setting up the ones that are relevant for you can slash your email time in half.

Social media posting. Tools like Hootsuite, Later, and Buffer let you manage multiple social media accounts and schedule posts. It's much more efficient to schedule a week of posts at once than to try to remember to go in and post every day.

Financial tools. Get those bills on autopay, set up automatic investments for your savings, and use budgeting apps to track where your money goes. This kicks that monthly financial mess to the curb while helping your money grow behind the scenes.

Household routines and subscriptions. Set up subscription deliveries for groceries, program your thermostat, let a robot vacuum handle the floors. These little automations keep your home life running without constant attention.

Strategy 2: Streamline common tasks.

While some tasks might not be completely automatable, they can often be streamlined. Consider:

Collaboration platforms. Tools like Microsoft Teams can help reduce the number of emails and the need for unnecessary meetings.

Calendar and reminder systems. Tools like Google Calendar or Calendly handle scheduling, reminders, and tasks that pop up regularly. Want to remember your buddy's birthday or that weekly check-in? Set it once and forget it!

Data entry. If you use tools like Excel and Google Sheets, a little education can help streamline data entry. For instance, have you learned how basic formulas and functions work? Or the tricks for repeating a series of numbers or dates? If you get a little further in, you might even learn how to set up macros to speed things up.

File management. Cloud storage tools like Dropbox or Google Drive can ensure easy access to your files from any location. Perhaps even more important is their backup function, ensuring that you don't lose important files if your computer ever crashes. Mine has—and gosh was I grateful for my online backup.

Strategy 3: Boost efficiency with assistance.

Easily accessible technology can also assist with somewhat more complicated tasks—and this area will only get more expansive, soon. Consider:

Digital assistants. Are you using Alexa, Siri, or Google Assistant for sending messages, reminders, and emails?

Artificial intelligence. If you have not yet been exposed to artificial intelligence, a.k.a. AI, you have a lot to look forward to! It is by far one of the twenty-first century's best tools for creating time affluence.

- AI can help you draft email messages, generate reports, or even recommend edits—which can save you hours!
- AI assistants can coordinate calendars and book meetings without endless back-and-forth communication.
- Your company can program AI chatbots to answer common questions instantly, reducing wait time for both staff and customers. The amazing part is that the person communicating with your AI chatbot often won't even know. Recently, I was scheduled to be interviewed by a podcaster and, unbeknownst to me, guess who scheduled and confirmed it: Yep! "Kaycee," the AI assistant!

Congratulations if you are already using some of these strategies—you're leveraging digital tools to save time. If not, it's never too late to incorporate these time-saving techniques into your routine.

Here's the real question: Now that you've freed up time, what will you do with it? Are you using your extra time for activities you enjoy, or have you filled those freed-up minutes with even more tasks?

Your Call to Action

Take a moment to reflect on how you are using technology in your daily life. Are you genuinely benefiting from the time it's supposed to save? Choose one or two of the strategies above and start implementing them today. Then, dedicate that extra time to something that enriches your life—relaxing, pursuing a hobby, or spending quality time with loved ones.

TIME AFFLUENCE TIP FROM A TOP CEO

Ryan Schefke, CEO of Lead Liaison, uses AI when he needs to move faster than his legal team can. For instance, he has ChatGPT review proposed contract changes from potential clients. The AI tool can spit out a redline document that identifies differences from the company's standard contract. "Show me the gaps, you know?" he explains. "It's a huge time saver. I cut our costs for legal probably by 90 percent, and I save the same amount of time."[50]

PART 6

Simplify and Streamline Life

STEP 23
Minimize Decision Fatigue

In any moment of decision, the best thing you can do
is the right thing, the next best thing is the wrong thing,
and the worst you can do is nothing.

THEODORE ROOSEVELT

Do you ever feel overwhelmed by the number of decisions you make in a single day? If you do, it's no wonder! While the number of decisions a person makes each day varies, it's higher than you might expect. Some sources put it at 35,000 decisions per day, 2,000 decisions per hour, or one decision every 2 seconds![51] That may sound as incredible to you as it did to me, but think about the number of decisions you made today. It may give more credence to this number. In fact, a study at Cornell University found that each day an individual makes almost 220 decisions about food and beverages alone.[52]

If you question these numbers, start listing the decisions you have made today, and you'll see how quickly they add up: the food you decided to eat, the clothes you decided to wear, how you decided to spend your day, and so on and so on.

How many decisions did you make? I counted the number of decisions I made today from the time I woke up until the time I began writing this piece: I decided to get up, brush my teeth, pet Mozart (our dog), sip water, pour coffee, call my daughter, schedule an eye appointment, order a book on Amazon, put on my running clothes, pack my workout bag, put my laptop in my workout bag, eat breakfast (including choosing what to eat), put on my winter coat, walk to the gym, exercise for 30 minutes, find a place to write, choose a seat, order coffee . . . I even decided whether to write on my laptop or my phone. If you count them, I made at least twenty decisions in a 2-hour period!

Have you gotten the picture that we all make an enormous number of decisions daily? While many of the decisions we make are real time zappers, they don't need to be. The goal of Step 23 is to help you minimize decision fatigue!

Seven Ways to Minimize Decision Fatigue

Anne Bogel, author of *How She Does It: An Everywoman's Guide to Breaking Old Rules, Getting Creative, and Making Time for Work in Your Actual, Everyday Life* and proprietor of the popular blog Modern Mrs. Darcy, offers seven practical strategies for women balancing work and personal life:

1. Eat the same thing. When I read this tip, I found it to be a ridiculous recommendation. When I looked at my eating habits, however, I realized that I had eaten the same thing for breakfast for the past year! Bogel was right; eating the same thing is one less decision to have to make.

2. . . . Or almost the same thing. Eating the same *kind* of food can actually be fun and also cut down on decisions. One of my dearest friends minimizes menu decisions by preparing the same type of food on a given day. Her weekly plan: Steak Sundays, Moussaka Mondays, Teriyaki Chicken Tuesdays, Whitefish Wednesdays, Taco Thursdays, Fillet of Sole Fridays, and Stew Saturdays.

3. Embrace daily routines. How would you describe your daily routine? What do you do the first hour of the day? What activities make up the last hour of your day? Most of us are creatures of habit. If you are one of them, you have minimized your decision fatigue by being on autopilot with at least part of your daily routine.

4. Establish hard edges in your day. If you have not established "hard edges" to your days, try it. What I mean is simply scheduling a beginning and end to your workday, and/or dedicating specific times of day to different activities. For instance, you may schedule meetings before 11:00 a.m., send correspondence between noon and 2:00 p.m., do proposals and invoices between 2:00 p.m. and 4:00 p.m., and tie up loose ends between 4:00 p.m. and 5:00 p.m. before calling it a day.

5. Create if-then rules for yourself. This guideline is a terrific way to avoid wasting energy on decision-making. If-then rules are a little like the habit stacking described in Step 10, with a trigger or cue, and a defined action to take—essentially you are making a decision in advance.

Here are four examples of what if-then rules look like:

- IF I have to choose between two similar options, THEN I will pick the one that aligns best with my long-term goals. Example: You're deciding between two job offers: one offers a higher salary, while the other provides opportunities for growth in your desired career path. You choose the latter, as it aligns with your long-term goal of advancing in that specific field.

- IF I feel overwhelmed by too many choices, THEN I will set a time limit of 10 minutes to decide. Example: While shopping online, you're inundated with numerous options for a new laptop. Feeling overwhelmed, you give yourself 10 minutes to review the top choices and make a decision, preventing prolonged indecision.

- IF I need to make a small decision, THEN I will default to my usual choice to avoid unnecessary deliberation. Example: Each morning, you spend time deciding what to have for breakfast. To streamline your routine, you decide that on weekdays, you'll default to oatmeal, saving time and mental energy.

- IF I am indecisive, THEN I will consult with a trusted friend or colleague for input. Example: You're uncertain about enrolling in a particular course. To gain clarity, you discuss it with a colleague who has taken the course, helping you make an informed decision.

Implementing these if-then rules can help reduce decision fatigue and streamline your daily choices. By establishing predetermined responses to common situations, you conserve mental energy and make more consistent decisions.

6. If it incites decision angst, drop it. We've all experienced anxiety when confronted with a decision. Bogel recommends controlling the situation rather than causing yourself mental exhaustion by feeling pressured to make the "right" decision, especially when there is no clear answer.

Here's a scenario that might cause decision fatigue unless you take control: You're invited to two events on the same night—a friend's casual dinner party and a networking mixer. You agonize over which to attend, weighing pros and cons until you feel paralyzed. Realizing that the stress isn't worth it, you decide to skip both and spend the evening relaxing at home, prioritizing your peace of mind instead.

7. Limit your options. To reduce decision fatigue, it's effective to narrow down the choices available when making a decision. This can mean something as simple as choosing a restaurant with a limited menu or committing in advance to ordering one of just three go-to entrees, like salmon, a hamburger, or steak. When you reduce the number of options to choose from, especially for routine decisions like what to eat, you conserve your mental energy for more important tasks. This approach transforms dining out from a source of stress into a small act of self-care. By narrowing your options ahead of time, you avoid the overwhelm of an endless menu and enjoy your meal with greater ease and satisfaction.[53]

Your Call to Action

Are you ready to reclaim your time and reduce the overwhelming decision fatigue in your life? Start today by implementing one or more of the strategies outlined above. Whether it's streamlining your meals, setting a hard edge on your workday, or creating if-then rules, these simple strategies can make a huge difference in how you manage your daily decisions.

TIME AFFLUENCE TIP FROM A TOP CEO

You might have noticed President Barack Obama had a consistent-looking wardrobe (except that one time with the tan suit!). He told Vanity Fair: *"You'll see I always wear only gray or blue suits. I'm trying to pare down decisions. I don't want to make decisions about what I'm eating or wearing. Because I have too many other decisions to make."*[54]

STEP 24
Declutter Your Space

I hate belongings. I hate clutter. It really bothers me because I can't think properly. If you've got distractions in front of you, your mind goes nuts.
SIMON COWELL

———————

Clutter. Let's face it: We all have it! Unless you're superhuman, you've probably wasted time searching for something that should have been easy to find. Did you forget where you placed it? Could you have lost it? Or was it due to that seven-letter word C-L-U-T-T-E-R?

While considering this step, I found myself wondering why we accumulate clutter—and what benefits decluttering might offer (besides saving time, of course!). It turns out that just as there's a psychology to why we cling to things, there's a psychology to the relief we feel when we let them go.

Let's get straight to the point without cluttering this section with unnecessary words.

Clutter, Clutter, Clutter

You don't need an advanced degree to know what clutter is. And it comes in many forms:

122

- **Paper clutter:** Bills, receipts, junk mail. Even in a digital age, many of us still wrestle with paper piles.
- **Clothing clutter:** That silk suit you've never worn, those aspirational jeans waiting for you to lose a few pounds, those mateless socks . . .
- **Sentimental clutter:** Gifts, cards, and mementos that tug at your heartstrings.
- **Digital clutter:** Invisible but mentally draining, it lives in your devices—old photos, emails, apps.

We all have a little clutter, but some of us are clutterbugs—champions of messiness. Symptoms of clutterbug syndrome:

- Owning clothes, electronics, or gadgets that haven't been used in over a year.
- Tossing random items in a junk drawer instead of discarding them.
- Having a catch-all guest room—with no room for guests!

The good news is, all of us—even us clutterbugs—can declutter.

All About Decluttering

Diane Roberts Stoler, Ed.D., highlights the mental benefits of decluttering in a 2023 *Psychology Today* article: Those who declutter often report clearer minds, less frustration, and increased productivity. In cluttered environments, people tend to feel overwhelmed, but removing clutter can boost self-esteem and focus.[55]

In short, decluttering isn't just about tidying your space—it's about clearing mental space for what truly matters. Think about it: Clutter competes for our attention, overwhelming the brain and increasing stress. When your home or work area is cluttered, it's harder to focus, solve problems, and feel at ease.

Decluttering helps to create a sense of control and accomplishment. Every small act of organizing gives your brain a hit of dopamine—that feel-good chemical—which boosts motivation and mood. It also reduces decision fatigue because you aren't constantly sorting through stuff to find what you need.

The bottom line: A tidy environment fosters a tidy mind. Less clutter equals less stress, more clarity, better time management, and more energy for what really matters.

Rate Yourself on the Clutter Scale

How do you measure up on the clutter scale? Take a close look at your personal environment and work environment and choose the number that best matches your current space.

1. Overwhelmed
- Environment: Piles of paper, messy desk, overflowing drawers, chaotic surfaces.
- Mental impact: High stress, easily distracted, low motivation.

2. Struggling
- Environment: Some organization, but pockets of clutter remain and feel distracting.
- Mental impact: Moderate stress, harder to stay focused.

3. Neutral
- Environment: A mix of clear and cluttered spaces, somewhat functional.
- Mental impact: Neutral mood, energy varies.

4. Focused
- Environment: Surfaces are mostly clear; clutter is minimal and organized.
- Mental impact: Increased calm, better concentration.

5. Energized
- Environment: Minimalist, organized, visually peaceful.
- Mental impact: High energy, strong focus, sense of control.

I hope you will use this as a tool to monitor your progress toward greater clarity and time affluence.

Tips for Quick Decluttering

While I can't add more hours to your day, I can help you reclaim time by tackling clutter in short, manageable bursts. Here are five tips that take no more than 1 minute each:

- At the end of each workday, clear your workspace of papers and extra items.
- Close computer tabs you won't need the following day.
- Recycle junk mail as soon as it arrives.
- Every time you open a cluttered drawer, discard at least one expired or unneeded item.
- Clean out your purse, briefcase, or duffle bag, and toss old receipts and junk.

By taking small steps, you put a dent in your clutter and gain momentum toward bigger efforts.

Decluttering Strategies

Ready for bigger action? Here are four simple strategies to get rid of those things that are taking up square footage in your home or office:

1. Set a decluttering deadline. Pick a firm deadline by which you want your space to feel lighter—whether it's one week or one month. Write it down, put it on your calendar, and treat it like an appointment you won't cancel.

2. Schedule decluttering time. Decide how often and for how long you'll declutter—15 minutes a day or 1 hour each weekend can make a big difference. Stick to the schedule so the task feels manageable, not overwhelming.

3. Use the "one category at a time" rule. Focus on one type of item at a time—books, clothes, papers, and so on—instead of trying to do an entire room at once. This helps you make faster, more consistent decisions.

4. Handle sentimental items last (and gently). Save sentimental things for the end when your decision-making muscles are stronger. Consider photographing items you're ready to part with so you can keep the memory without keeping the object.

Rather than make decluttering one massive project, start with 5 minutes a day. Quick wins will make decluttering less stressful. The more you clear out, the more space you will make in your life for what matters.

When You Cannot Get Yourself to Begin Decluttering

Even if you have the best intentions, you may find yourself procrastinating on decluttering. Here are five quick, effective ways to motivate yourself to declutter your home or office:

1. Visualize the outcome. Picture how calm, spacious, and organized your space will feel once it's decluttered. This positive mental image can spark the motivation to start.

2. Set small, achievable goals. Break down the task into tiny steps, like clearing just one drawer or one shelf. Small wins build momentum and keep you encouraged.

3. Remember the benefits. Decluttering reduces stress, boosts productivity, and makes it easier to find what you need. Keeping these benefits in mind helps maintain your drive.

4. Reward yourself. Plan a small treat after completing a decluttering session—like your favorite coffee or a short walk. Rewards make the process feel worthwhile.

5. Invite support. Ask a friend or family member to help or simply cheer you on. Having company can make the task more enjoyable and less daunting.

Decluttering isn't just about tidying up—it's about creating space for clarity, focus, and peace of mind. Start small, stay consistent, and remind yourself that every item you let go of brings you closer to a more intentional and inspiring environment.

Your Call to Action

Clear your space, clear your mind! Start today: Choose one drawer, one shelf, or one bag. Take 5 minutes to remove what you don't need. Keep only what energizes you and will save you time in the long run.

TIME AFFLUENCE TIP FROM A TOP CEO

Elmer Smith, who served as president of Southern Ohio College in the early 1980s, was adamant about his team having their desks cleared off at the end of each workday. He insisted that each person dedicate a desk drawer in which to put ongoing projects. I know for a fact that this CEO "walked the talk"—because I worked for him!

STEP 25
Streamline Your Dressing Routine

Choosing a streamlined wardrobe is like giving yourself extra minutes every morning—a small act that adds up to more time for what truly matters.

UNKNOWN

———————

Have you ever timed how long it takes you to get dressed? (Men, I'm talking to you too!)

I hadn't considered timing my dressing routine until I read the results of a survey conducted by Marks and Spencer (M&S), a major British retailer. The survey of 2,000 men and women revealed that the average time to get dressed is 17 minutes, which amounts to approximately *four days* a year. To put it in perspective, if you lived to age 89, you would have spent nearly one year of your life getting dressed!

The study found that most individuals take between 11 and 30 minutes to get ready. Only 2 percent reported taking less than 5 minutes, while 3 percent admitted to taking over an hour.

Who do you think takes longer to get dressed: men or women? You guessed it—women! According to this survey, 21 percent of men take more than 30 minutes, compared to 38 percent of women. Sixteen percent of women surveyed said they wear makeup every day, while 32 percent wear it most days, which may contribute to the longer dressing time.[56]

While the M&S study is far from scientific, it offers a glimpse into the average dressing times of people. Personally, when dressing casually, I can throw on a pair of slacks and a top in about 10 minutes. However, like many, I tend to invest more time in choosing outfits for work or special occasions, often going through a "dress rehearsal" beforehand.

Quiz: How Long Does It Take You to Get Dressed?

Before I share five ways to streamline your dressing time, I invite you to take an eight-point quiz to assess your getting-dressed habits.

DIRECTIONS

Circle the letter that best reflects your experience.

1. How frequently do you plan what you are going to wear the following day before you go to bed?
   A. Always. It's the last thing I do before sleep.
   B. I think about it, but if I get home late, I'm often too tired to plan.
   C. No way!

2. How organized is your closet?
   A. It's organized by category.
   B. I have a general idea of where things are.
   C. It's one big mess!

3. How often do you wear the same outfit combinations?
   A. More often than I'd like to admit!
   B. Occasionally; I get bored with the same clothes.
   C. Hardly ever; I love wearing different outfits.

4. How quickly can you accessorize your clothes?
   A. Quick as a bunny; I wear the same accessories every day.
   B. I try on a few items before deciding.
   C. It takes way too long; I send pictures to my sister for help!

5. What is your grooming routine like in the morning?
   A. It's quick; I splash water on my face and use five items to look and smell good.
   B. My daily toiletries are easily accessible.
   C. I spend more time than necessary on grooming.

6. How long does it take to put on your shoes?
   A. Less than a minute.
   B. A few minutes for stylish boots that zip.
   C. Five minutes if I'm wearing complicated shoes.

7. Do you use apps to plan your outfits?
   A. I have pictures of ten favorite outfits to simplify my mornings.
   B. I've considered using an app.
   C. Never.

8. Do you schedule a certain amount of time to get dressed?
   A. I give myself a maximum of 15 minutes.
   B. Rarely.
   C. I see getting dressed as leisure time, so I take my time.

HOW DID YOU SCORE?
Give yourself:
- 1 point for every A
- 2 points for every B
- 3 points for every C

If you scored:

- **8 to 12 points:** You are quick and efficient (5 to 10 minutes). You've mastered the art of getting dressed and are a role model for others!
- **13 to 18 points:** You take a moderate amount of time (10 to 15 minutes). Consider laying out your clothes the night before and opting for slip-on shoes and simple accessories.
- **19 to 24 points:** You take your time (15+ minutes). If you enjoy taking your time dressing, that's perfectly fine. However, if you want to save time, put together five go-to outfits and enjoy primping with shoes and accessories.

Five Ways to Save Time Getting Ready

From decluttering your closet to categorizing your wardrobe by season, there are numerous strategies to reduce the time spent getting dressed. Here are five effective ways to streamline your dressing routine:

1. Declutter your dressing area. If you haven't worn a piece of clothing or an accessory in two years, consider donating it. This doesn't apply to heirlooms, of course, but rather items that don't fit or that you haven't worn. If you can't part with something, create a donation box and store it away. In six months, if you haven't missed it, donate it. You can also wash, iron, or dry-clean items for consignment. Don't take it personally if they reject your clothes because they're "too loved"—that just means they're too worn out!

2. Categorize your closet by season. Store seasonal clothing that you won't wear for the next few months out of sight. This could mean placing them at the back of your closet, in a spare room closet, or in a bin under your bed. You'll be amazed at how much space you create for the items you actually wear.

3. Create grab-and-go outfits. Now that you've decluttered, lay out clothes intended for work or leisure. Assemble five work outfits with your favorite tops and bottoms. Add a scarf or necktie, and hang these complete outfits together in your closet. This will save you from having to figure out what goes with what each morning—your only decisions will be shoes and accessories.

4. Do a dress rehearsal. If you want to incorporate clothes you haven't worn in a while, set aside a rainy weekend for a dress rehearsal. Trying on outfits ahead of time means you won't have to think twice about what to wear when the time comes.

5. Have a few sizeless outfits. Let's face it: Some days you may feel bloated or in some way physically uncomfortable. Rather than stressing, in one of your grab-and-go ensembles, include a skirt or pair of slacks that fit comfortably regardless of the day's challenges.

Streamlining your wardrobe isn't about having less; it's more about making what you have work for you. By organizing your space, you may find that getting dressed is less stressful. A few changes can turn those chaotic mornings into calm starts of the day.

Your Call to Action

Now that you have the tools to streamline your dressing routine, it's time to act! Start by assessing your closet this weekend. Declutter, organize, and create those grab-and-go outfits. Share your progress and tips with friends or family and inspire them to join you in making mornings more efficient.

TIME AFFLUENCE TIP FROM A TOP CEO

Georgette Mosbacher, former chairman and CEO of La Prairie, shared in her book Feminine Force *that she often had the same suits or outfits tailored in different colors as a way of streamlining her wardrobe. Besides providing consistency in her appearance, this approach was part of Mosbacher's signature fashion style, which blended practicality with elegance.* [57]

STEP 26
Turn Off Default Notifications

There are always distractions, if you allow them.
**TONY LA RUSSA, FORMER PROFESSIONAL BASEBALL PLAYER,
COACH, AND MANAGER**

―――――――
―――――

There's no doubt about it! Pings, buzzes, and flashes consume a large part of our lives. While many of these external distractions are difficult to control, a few can be managed: email message pop-ups, social media alerts, and other such default notifications.

According to a 2024 TeamStage article, smartphones, the internet, and checking social media are among the biggest distractions at work.[58] The same article suggests the most effective way to manage such mental interruptions is simple: Turn off your phone and avoid checking emails until you finish the project at hand.

If you need more convincing beyond this commonsense approach to avoid being distracted by nonessential push notifications, let me share advice from Jill Duffy, *PCMag*'s Get Organized columnist. She advises that the only notifications you should leave on are the ones you are going to do something about the moment they arrive. These might include messaging apps, calendars, baby monitors, smart home security systems, and rideshare apps.

Duffy also offers five practical recommendations:

1. Turn off all nonessential push notifications. Unless you need them for work, turn off news pushes, social media alerts, notifications from shopping apps, and so on. Note: You can customize notifications so that you see them when you *open* your phone.

2. Mute nonessential threads and chains. Duffy suggests that while certain channels like Slack, WhatsApp, and Discord may be much-needed notifications in your life, muting them will increase the signal-to-noise ratio by cutting out "noise."

3. Set reminders 2 minutes before meetings. While 2 minutes is not enough time for me, Duffy advocates 2 minutes as an alert to wrap up the task at hand and sign in to a scheduled virtual meeting. As for in-person meetings, set your alert 1 to 2 hours before the scheduled time.

4. Worst case travel time plus 10 minutes. Duffy suggests this equation for out-of-office meetings, but she must move faster than the speed of light; even as a seasoned minute master, I advocate travel time plus 30 minutes (rather than 10 minutes)!

5. Use color, bold, and all caps . . . sparingly! Duffy recommends using color, bold, and all caps infrequently in your calendar and notifications so they stand out when they do appear. When overused, these elements risk losing their impact. She's right—too much of anything dilutes the intended effect.[59]

Small adjustments to how you manage notifications, meetings, and alerts can make a big difference in reducing daily distractions. Duffy's tips are easy to implement and a powerful way to help you stay focused. By turning off push notifications, your digital tools can work *for* you rather than *against* you.

Push Notifications Affect Your Productivity

If you have even an iota of doubt that push notifications affect your productivity, think again. Numerous studies have been done on the impact that distractions have, and they clearly show how much more productive people are when they are not interrupted. Hungarian American psychologist Mihaly Csikszentmihalyi introduced the concept of *flow*, meaning complete immersion in a task. Flow is important because it's the state in which people do their best work and feel most fulfilled. When "in the flow," you are fully focused, perform at a higher level, and experience a sense of enjoyment that makes work feel more meaningful.

In a 2019 *Harvard Business Review* article, Steve Glaveski writes that push notifications block our ability to get into flow. Instead, he says, we become like Pavlov's dogs, conditioned to immediately react.[60]

In fact, according to a study conducted by Gloria Mark, professor and researcher at the University of California, Irvine, workers spend on average only 10 minutes and 30 seconds on a task before being interrupted. Professor Mark found that while 56 percent of interruptions were from an external source, self-interruption occurred a whopping 44 percent of the time. Even worse, when we switch tasks after reading an unexpected incoming notification, it can take 23 minutes and 15 seconds to get back to the task at hand.[61]

Ultimately, notifications exploit our brain's craving for novelty and affirmation, pulling us away from focused work before we even realize it.

Quiz: How Well Do You Manage Default Notifications?

Now that you have read about how you can be more productive by better managing default notifications, take a closer look at how you are managing them in your daily life. Your responses to the quiz below will help you to see if you are a notification ninja or in digital chaos.

DIRECTIONS
Circle the letter that best reflects your experience.

1. How often do you adjust notification settings on new apps?
   A. Always—it's the first thing I do!
   B. Occasionally, if notifications get overwhelming.
   C. Rarely—I usually stick with default settings.
   D. Never—I didn't even know you could adjust them.

2. When a notification pops up while you're working, what do you do?
   A. Ignore it until I'm done.
   B. Glance at it quickly, then refocus.
   C. Check it and maybe respond before getting back to work.
   D. Get distracted and forget what I was doing.

3. How many apps currently send you notifications?
   A. 5 or fewer—only the essentials.
   B. 6 to 10—I've narrowed it down, but there's still room to improve.
   C. 11 to 20—there are too many, but I deal with it.
   D. 20+—I'm drowning in notifications!

4. What's your approach to group chat notifications?
   A. Mute them unless they're important.
   B. Leave them on for work; mute personal ones.
   C. Let all notifications come through—FOMO is real!
   D. Keep them on but feel overwhelmed constantly.

5. Do you use Do Not Disturb (or Focus) mode?
   A. Yes, every day—it's a lifesaver!
   B. Occasionally, when I really need to concentrate.
   C. Rarely—only if I'm in a meeting or driving.
   D. Never—I don't know how to set it up.

6. How often do you do a notification declutter (that is, review and adjust settings)?
   A. Monthly—I stay on top of it.
   B. Every few months, when I notice issues.
   C. Once a year, if that.
   D. Never—I just deal with the chaos.

7. How do you feel when you hear your phone's notification sound?
   A. Indifferent—I rarely hear it since I manage notifications well.
   B. Slightly annoyed—I get more than I'd like.
   C. Stressed—it feels like an interruption.
   D. Overwhelmed—it's constant!

HOW DID YOU SCORE?

To determine your score, give yourself:
- 1 point for every A
- 2 points for every B
- 3 points for every C
- 4 points for every D

What your score indicates:
- **7 to 10 points: Notification Ninja.** You're in control! Notifications don't rule your life, and you know how to keep distractions to a minimum.
- **11 to 17 points: Balanced User.** You've got a good handle on notifications, but there's room to refine your system for better focus and peace of mind.
- **18 to 24 points: Notification Overload.** Notifications are starting to take over. Consider decluttering your settings and using features like Do Not Disturb.
- **25+ points: Digital Chaos.** It's time for an intervention! Take control of your notifications to reclaim time and reduce stress.

Your Call to Action

Regain control of your attention and reduce digital overwhelm by turning off all nonessential notifications on your phone and computer—news alerts, social media pings, shopping app buzzes. Keep only notifications that are truly urgent or essential, such as work-related calls or messages from family.

TIME AFFLUENCE TIP FROM A TOP CEO

Matt Sonnen, COO at Coldstream Wealth Management, says, "Several years ago, I turned off email notifications because I was regularly finding myself missing critical information during Zoom calls because an email pop-up in the bottom corner of my screen sent my mind in four or five different directions."[62]

STEP 27
Unplug from Technology

Figure out a way to set limits so you can concentrate when you need to, and disengage when you need to. Technology is a good servant but a bad master.
GRETCHEN RUBIN, AUTHOR OF *OUTER ORDER, INNER CALM*

———————

What would we do without technology? It's an indispensable tool, yet it has created a digital dilemma. If you're like most people, your devices have become extensions of your body and mind. Perhaps you've noticed it in others even more than in yourself.

According to former US Surgeon General Vivek Murthy, we're in the midst of a "loneliness epidemic," fueled in part by our constant connectivity to technology. Are you unknowingly contributing to this epidemic?[63]

According to a 2024 Pew Research Center article, about 4 in 10 Americans report being online almost constantly.[64] If you're one of the 40 percent constantly plugged in, a digital detox might be exactly what you need to regain time and peace of mind.

You may not think you need a digital detox, but ask yourself: When was the last time you were in a meeting or restaurant and were more focused on your phone's messages than the people around you?

Or, think of the last time you observed people at a restaurant. Did you notice a family at the next table, each member glued to their own device? The child entertained by a video, the preteen absorbed in a game, parents texting their bosses—this has become the new normal.

Before we point fingers at others, let's look at ourselves. Could we, too, benefit from unplugging?

Quiz: Do You Need a Digital Detox?

Take this short quiz to evaluate how much time you spend online versus offline. I took it too, and I'll share my results after you complete the quiz.

DIRECTIONS

Circle the letter that best reflects your experience.

1. How much time do you spend on social media each day?
    A. Less than 1 hour
    B. 1 to 2 hours
    C. 3 to 5 hours
    D. More than 5 hours

2. How often do you check your phone within an hour?
    A. Rarely
    B. Once or twice
    C. Several times
    D. I'm constantly checking it

3. When was the last time you spent a day without using the internet or digital devices?
    A. Within the past week
    B. Within the past month
    C. A few months ago
    D. I can't remember

4. How do you feel when you're offline for more than an hour?
   A. Free and relaxed
   B. Slightly out of touch
   C. Bored to death
   D. I never stay offline for that long

5. How often do you take time to read, exercise, or do something just for fun?
   A. Daily
   B. A few times a week
   C. Once a week or less
   D. Rarely or never

HOW DID YOU SCORE?

If most of your answers are A's, congratulations! You're maintaining a healthy balance between online and offline time.

If your answers are mostly B's, you're doing okay, but you may be at risk of sliding into digital overload without realizing it. Your habits aren't extreme, but they may be crowding out more restorative or creative activities. Consider experimenting with a short daily screen break, or try turning off notifications to regain control of your attention.

If your answers lean toward C's or D's, it might be time to consider a digital detox.

As promised, let me share my results. To the four questions, I scored one A, two C's and one D—which simply confirmed that I am in dire need of a digital detox. I scheduled one for this weekend. What about you?

Signs You Need a Digital Detox

Not sure the numbers tell the whole story? Here are six symptoms that point to the need for a digital detox:

1. You feel anxious or stressed without your phone. If even short breaks from your device make you uncomfortable, that's a big clue.

2. You constantly check your devices without a real reason. Opening apps out of habit—not because you need something—suggests digital overuse.

3. Your sleep is suffering. Difficulty falling asleep, waking up often, or feeling exhausted in the morning can be linked to too much screen time, especially before bed.

4. You feel less connected to people in real life. If online interactions start to feel easier or more frequent than in-person ones, it could be time to rebalance.

5. You have trouble focusing. If it's hard to concentrate for even a few minutes without reaching for your phone, your attention span might be shrinking.

6. You experience phantom vibrations. Thinking you hear or feel your phone when it hasn't buzzed is a real phenomenon—and a signal that you might need a break.

If these signs sound familiar, your mind might be ready for a digital detox. It doesn't have to be drastic; it can start with small breaks that may help you reconnect with yourself and those around you. Try giving your brain some space to rest; you may be surprised by how much more focused you feel.

The Value of Unplugging

As someone who was overdue for a digital detox and finally took one, I can tell you that there are at least four strong benefits to doing it.

1. Stronger personal relationships. When stepping away from devices, you naturally make more time for real-world conversations and experiences. This strengthens your emotional connections with family, friends, and even yourself.

2. Improved mental health. Spending less time online, especially on social media, can lower anxiety and stress and reduce feelings of loneliness. A digital detox helps reset your brain, giving you space to think more clearly and feel more grounded.

3. Better sleep quality. Screens emit blue light that can disrupt your natural sleep-wake cycle (circadian rhythm). By reducing screen time—especially before bed—you can fall asleep faster, sleep deeper, and wake up feeling refreshed.

4. Increased focus and productivity. Constant notifications and multi-tasking online scatter your attention. Taking a break from digital distractions boosts your ability to focus deeply on tasks, solve problems creatively, and finish work more efficiently—often with less stress.

If you could use improvement in these areas, it might be time to reassess your relationship with technology. A digital detox does not have to be extreme. Even small detox breaks can help you feel more focused, rested, and connected. Your goal does not need to be giving up your devices; your focus should be to make sure you are in charge of them rather than they you.

Detox Gently!

If you're ready to unplug, take it slowly and methodically. A sudden detox can be overwhelming. Follow this approach adapted from "Digital Detox: How to Unplug and Recharge, A Step-by-Step Guide":

1. Assess your digital dependence. Acknowledge how much time you spend online. Only then can you begin to cut back.

2. Set specific goals. Decide which habits to break. Maybe you'll stop texting while walking, or not sleep with your phone beside you.

3. Unplug gradually. Start small. Perhaps delay checking your devices until after you have dressed in the morning, or designate one tech-free day during the weekend.

4. Create tech-free zones. Identify times or areas you won't use devices, like during meals or meetings or in the bedroom.

5. Mix it up. Rather than consuming all information digitally, try reading a physical book or picking up a magazine.[65]

Unplugging can be refreshing, but prepare ahead of time. Decide how you'll fill the extra hours. Will you take a walk, meditate, or spend more time reading? Plan activities that will help you recharge, connect with yourself, and foster real connections with others.

Your Call to Action

Ready to reclaim your time and mental clarity? Start by assessing your current technology habits. You might be surprised by what you uncover—and awareness is the first step toward change.

TIME AFFLUENCE TIP FROM A TOP CEO

Tommie Edwards, founder of Eventbree, says, "On one day I'll turn my phone on airplane mode for 3 or 4 hours to concentrate and make critical decisions without any distraction. On other days, I stay off social media and emails for a few hours by turning off their notifications."[66]

STEP 28
Set Tech-Free Zones at Home and at Work

The good and the wise lead quiet lives.

EURIPIDES

––––––––––

In Step 27, you learned an important way to enhance your time affluence by doing a digital detox. Realistically speaking, however, there is a good chance that you will regress to your old habits with your tech tools.

You don't need research to tell you that it's easier to focus when your phone is out of sight. Seriously! I know firsthand that even when my phone is turned off or face down on the table, its mere *presence* seems to reduce my cognitive capacity. I guess it is because my brain remains subconsciously alert to notifications, messages, and other interactions.

If it is not already mandated in the locations you frequent, give serious thought to minimizing distractions by creating tech-free areas in your life—whether by time, event, or location. Below you'll find the five tech-free areas that I imposed upon myself. To avoid having withdrawal symptoms, I introduced one per week over a two-month period.

1. Bedroom. I redefined this room as my sanctuary for rest and connection.

2. Dining table. I find that screen-free meals encourage mindfulness when I'm alone and more meaningful conversations when I'm with family or others.

3. Car, especially when driving. This is an important one for safety if nothing else. I finally stopped my sneak peeks at the screen when I put my purse with my phone in the back seat.

4. Social gatherings. To avoid looking (and being) rude, I shut my phone before entering a gathering. It helps me to focus on meeting new people and the conversation at hand.

5. Outdoor areas. Whether walking down the street or strolling through Central Park, I have become much more aware of my surroundings and nature.

Ask yourself which environments you are willing to designate as tech-free areas in your life—or at least where you are willing to detach from your smartphone:

- During meals with family and friends
- During social interaction
- During walks
- During low-tech activities
- In the bathroom
- In your bedroom
- When you are driving, except when listening to a podcast or audiobook

Select your device-free areas in environments where you would like to concentrate, recharge, and relax.

Where Tech-Free Environments Already Exist

Some tech-free environments already exist. For instance:

Private clubs. Some private social and business clubs limit the use of technology. I belong to a private club that bans cell phone use in the building. The protocol is for club members and guests to step into designated phone booths to make calls, return voice mail messages, or send texts.

Schools. Schools across the US have started banning cell phones during class. One is Kansas City's Ewing Marion Kauffman School. When students entered their classrooms in September 2024, they found cell phone lockboxes awaiting them. That's right—this school's policy requires that all high school students lock away their phones for the day. The reason: A pilot study was conducted in 2023 with one ninth-grade class. According to Deon Whitten, dean of students, the phone-free students had the highest GPAs across the board.[67] Ohio, Indiana, Oklahoma, and Florida have imposed statewide restrictions on the use of smartphones in public schools. According to social psychologist Jonathan Haidt, a major reason for implementing such measures is the strong link between smartphone use and declining mental health.[68]

Restaurants. Some dining establishments across the globe believe that dining without your phone makes the meal taste better. In fact, as of this writing, Al Condominio in Verona, Italy, offers a free bottle of wine to guests who lock away their cell phone during a meal. And at Caterina's in Fort Worth, Texas, diners must put their phone in a bag.[69]

From classrooms to clubs to candlelit dinners, more places are recognizing the value of disconnecting from devices. These tech-free zones remind us that presence, focus, and human connection still matter deeply. Perhaps we all should create more of these spaces in our lives.

Your Call to Action

If you're feeling overwhelmed by constant screen time, set up tech-free zones in your life. Designate spaces like your bedroom, dining area, or even cozy reading room as areas where your digital devices are off-limits. Use your tech-free time to relax, think, meditate, or simply recharge. Start small by committing to one tech-free area today—and see the difference it makes.

TIME AFFLUENCE TIP FROM A TOP CEO

In 2017, Bill Gates, legendary founder of the world's largest software firm, told the Mirror, *the popular British national daily tabloid, with respect to his kids: "We often set a time after which there is no screen time and in their case that helps them get to sleep at a reasonable hour."*[70]

PART 7

Build Time Affluence for Life

STEP 29
Learn to Deal with Setbacks

The comeback is always stronger than the setback.

ANONYMOUS

———————

No matter how well you plan or how disciplined you are, life will throw you curveballs. A perfectly crafted schedule can unravel in moments due to unexpected demands, personal challenges, or even just an off day. Setbacks are inevitable, but they don't have to derail your journey toward time affluence. In fact, learning how to recover from setbacks is one of the most powerful time-affluent skills you can develop.

Why Setbacks Happen

Before diving into recovery strategies, it's important to understand the root causes of setbacks.

Common triggers include:

- **Overcommitting:** Did you take on more tasks than your schedule could handle?
- **Unrealistic planning:** Should you be leaving more buffer time for unexpected delays?
- **External disruptions:** Did you encounter last-minute meetings or interruptions?

- **Internal challenges:** Did you find yourself procrastinating, or were you demotivated or tired?

Recognizing your own patterns may help you anticipate and mitigate future setbacks before they happen.

Recovering from a Setback

Time-affluent individuals view setbacks as opportunities to learn, not reasons to quit. Does that describe you? In other words, rather than fixating on what went wrong, are you focused on how to move forward? This shift in mindset is crucial. For example, instead of saying "I've failed at this routine again; I'll never get it right," develop the mindset "This setback shows me what needs to be adjusted to make my system stronger."

When you have that mindset in place, it makes individual setbacks easier to handle. Here are five steps to recover from a setback:

1. Pause and reflect. Give yourself a moment to acknowledge the setback in a constructive way by asking yourself:

- What happened?
- Was this within my control, or beyond my control?
- What can I learn from this experience?

Example: If you missed your morning planning session, was it because of a late night or an urgent morning meeting?

2. Revisit your goals. Setbacks can make us lose sight of our *why*. Reconnect with your purpose:

- Why is time affluence important to you?
- What are the long-term benefits you're working toward?

Pro Tip: Write down your top three time affluence goals and keep them somewhere visible as a daily reminder.

3. Start small to regain momentum. Are you overwhelmed by how far you've strayed? If so, perhaps you should start with a small, manageable action:

154

- Declutter your workspace for 5 minutes.
- Create a short to-do list for the day.
- Complete one high-priority task.

Example: After a chaotic week, focus on writing down just two priorities for the following day.

4. Adjust your strategies. Setbacks often highlight where your system needs flexibility:

- Am I too rigid? Should I add buffer time between tasks?
- Am I overly ambitious? Should I scale down my daily goals?
- Am I too easily interrupted? Should I set clearer boundaries?

5. Celebrate recovery. Recognize that bouncing back itself is a win. Treat yourself to something small—an uninterrupted walk, a favorite snack, or a guilt-free TV break.

Preventative Tips: Reducing Future Setbacks

While you can't eliminate all setbacks, you can make them less likely:

- **Plan buffer time.** Add 15 to 30 minutes between major tasks.
- **Simplify your schedule.** Prioritize two to three key tasks daily.
- **Track patterns.** Keep a journal to identify recurring challenges.
- **Check your energy.** Schedule demanding tasks during your most productive hours.

Small changes today can help prevent bigger disruptions tomorrow. By proactively managing your time, energy, and expectations, you will build resilience into your routine. Start with one of the tips above and see how it makes a difference.

Your Call to Action

Setbacks are not failures; they are opportunities to refine your approach. The path to time affluence isn't a straight line—it's a journey filled with lessons. Each time you recover, you're building resilience and getting closer to the life you want. After your next setback, try the five recovery steps outlined above. Write down what worked, what didn't, and how you'll adapt moving forward.

Time affluence is less about perfection and more about persistence. Keep going—you're making progress, 1 minute at a time!

TIME AFFLUENCE TIP FROM A TOP CEO

Tim Cook, CEO of Apple, embraces a "fail fast, learn faster" mentality, ensuring that setbacks don't take up excessive time. He focuses on how to recover quickly and move on to the next challenge.[71]

STEP 30
Be Available for What (and Who) Matters Most

If you've made it to this point, take a few minutes to appreciate what that means. Could it be that you are thinking differently about your time?

You've begun saying no when it matters. You've stopped letting urgency dictate your day. You're starting to see time less as something to conquer and more as something to shape—with clarity, care, and intention.

So now that we are at the final step in this book, let me ask you a question: What truly matters to you?

Time affluence isn't about crossing everything off your list. It doesn't depend on perfect systems or color-coded calendars. It's something deeper. It's the growing confidence that you get to decide how your time is spent. And now you're ready to decide with purpose.

Before you turn the page or close this book, here's a small invitation:

- Think of three people who help you feel like yourself—people who bring calm or laughter or who remind you what matters.
- Now think of three things that restore you. Not responsibilities, but activities that make you feel fully alive—cooking slowly, walking in nature, singing loudly in the car, laughing until you lose track of the time.
- Next, look at your calendar. Find time for one of those people and one of those joys. Rather than doing it out of obligation, do it because you want to do so.

Time affluence doesn't have a finish line. It's not about doing less—it's about making space for what's most meaningful and for who is most important.

Your Call to Action

Pause here for 10 minutes. Breathe deeply. Take stock. Write down:
- Three people you'd love to spend more meaningful time with.
- Three activities that light you up—your small, personal sources of joy.

Choose one from each list. Look at the week ahead. Block out time, even if it's just 15 minutes. Protect that time. This isn't extra; this is the good stuff. This is what we're learning to prioritize.

TIME AFFLUENCE TIP FROM A TOP CEO

Kasper Rørsted, former CEO of Adidas, was known for how deliberately he managed his time. He left the office by 6:00 p.m., carved out regular time for exercise, and kept weekends for his family. He didn't see these boundaries as luxuries. He saw them as essential to good leadership. "I think your return becomes dilutive the more time you spend," he once said.[72] His example is a reminder: Protecting your time isn't indulgent. It's powerful. It allows you to show up fully—for others and for yourself.

CLOSING THOUGHTS
Time Is Your Wealth

By now, you've probably realized this book was never about maximizing productivity. It was about creating more space in your day, your thoughts, and your life.

Time affluence doesn't require waking up earlier or adding more to your day. It simply asks you to pause long enough to notice what's important, and then give yourself the freedom to choose it.

You don't need to become a different person. You don't need a radical new routine. You just need to keep asking yourself, gently and honestly: Is this how I want to spend my time?

That one question can shift everything.

And when you begin treating your time as something valuable, you start remembering how valuable your life is too.

So take a breath. Think of the people, the places, and the little moments that bring you back to yourself.

Go toward them. Even for just 5 minutes.

I'd Love to Hear from You

If this book has shifted anything for you, I hope you'll share it. Maybe you've started carving out quiet mornings. Maybe you're finally making time for something that's been weighing on your heart. Whatever your story, I'd love to hear it.

Email me at annmarie@annmariesabath.com or tag me online with #TimeAffluent.

Time isn't just something we manage. It's something we share. And your story could be just the encouragement someone else needs to take their first step.

EXERCISES

Want to put these 30 steps to time affluence into practice?

To assist you in giving yourself more time, what follows are companion exercises to assist you in becoming the minute master of *your* time.

These aren't assignments. They're gentle tools—invitations, really—to help you make time affluence part of your daily life. Whether it's naming your personal time thieves, setting clearer boundaries, or carving out moments for joy, each exercise is practical, doable, and aligned with the step's core idea.

Let them be your next small step toward regaining control of your time.

EXERCISES FOR STEP 1
Understand How You Value Time

Understanding the true worth of your time can profoundly impact your priorities and decisions. The following exercises are designed to help you evaluate how you regard your time and align it with your goals and values.

Exercise 1: Assign a Dollar Value to Your Time

Ask yourself: How much do you believe an hour of your time is worth? Multiply your answer by 40 hours per week and 52 weeks per year. Compare this figure to your current income. Does the way you spend your time reflect what you believe it is worth?

Exercise 2: Create a Time Audit

For one week, track how you spend each hour of your day. Use categories such as work, family time, hobbies, relaxation, and errands. At the end of the week, analyze how much time you devote to each category, and determine whether your time allocation reflects your priorities.

Exercise 3: Identify What Makes You Feel Wealthy

Write a short paragraph describing what makes you feel rich—time with loved ones, financial security, or other factors. Reflect on whether your current lifestyle supports this feeling of wealth.

Exercise 4: Weigh Time-vs.-Money Decisions

Think about a recent decision where you had to choose between saving time and saving money. For example: Did you pay for convenience, such as food delivery, or spend time to save money by cooking at home? Write down how you made your choice and whether you were satisfied with the outcome.

Exercise 5: Design Your Ideal Day

Describe a day where you spend time exactly as you'd like. Include time for work, leisure, relationships, and self-care. Reflect on how closely your current days align with this vision and what changes you could make.

EXERCISES FOR STEP 2
Identify Your Time Personality

These exercises are meant to help you understand your time personality and to see how you manage (or don't manage) your time. By identifying both your strengths and challenges, you may find yourself making more intentional choices that will support your goals.

Exercise 1: Goal Setting for Growth

Write a specific goal to enhance your time management based on your personality type. For example:

- **Procrastinator:** Break tasks into smaller, actionable steps.
- **Multitasker:** Concentrate on completing one task at a time.
- **Planner:** Introduce flexibility into your daily routine.
- **Free Spirit:** Add structure to your schedule.

Track your progress on this goal for one week. Reflect on your results to assess areas of improvement and continued growth.

Exercise 2: Strengths and Challenges Chart

Create a two-column chart with the headings Strengths and Challenges. Based on your time personality, list three to five time management strengths in the first column. In the second column, list time management areas where you face challenges. After completing the chart, identify one challenge to focus on improving over the coming week.

EXERCISES FOR STEP 3

Identify Your Most Productive Time of Day

Everyone has natural energy peaks and dips throughout the day. The following exercises are meant to assist you in discovering when you are at your best. By identifying your peak energy times, you may better align your tasks with your personal rhythms.

Exercise 1: Circadian Rhythm Discovery

For one week, observe when you naturally wake up and feel tired without using alarms or external influences (if feasible). Note any variations and align your daily activities to these rhythms.

Exercise 2: End-of-Day Reflection

A daily reflection can give you a deeper understanding of your productivity rhythm over time. For one week, at the end of each day, answer these questions:
- What time of day felt most productive and why?
- Were there specific distractions or challenges that influenced your energy?
- How did your energy change as the day progressed?

Identify any consistent trends.

Exercise 3: Productivity Experiment

If you're not sure when your most productive times are, try an experiment.

1. Choose three types of tasks: creative tasks (e.g., brainstorming, writing), analytical tasks (e.g., data analysis, problemsolving), and routine tasks (e.g., emails, filing).

2. Perform each type of task during different times of the day (e.g., morning, afternoon, evening).

3. Assess your performance: How quickly did you complete the task? How satisfied were you with the outcome? Did it feel easier or harder depending on the time?

Exercise 4: Create a Personalized Task Schedule

Aligning your tasks with your natural energy patterns optimizes both efficiency and satisfaction. Based on your observations from prior exercises, assign tasks to the times of day when you're most effective, for instance:

- Morning: High-focus tasks (e.g., strategic planning, creative work)
- Afternoon: Moderate-focus tasks (e.g., meetings, administrative work)
- Evening: Low-focus tasks (e.g., folding laundry, watering plants, scrolling social media)

Follow this schedule for a week, and adjust as necessary.

EXERCISES FOR STEP 4

Schedule a Minimum of 2 Hours of Free Time Each Day

Incorporate these exercises into your daily schedule to ensure you dedicate at least 2 hours of free time to yourself. Use the suggested time slots or adjust them to fit your routine. By practicing these exercises and reflecting daily, you'll soon master the art of carving out personal time and reaping its benefits.

Exercise 1: Morning Reset (30 Minutes)

Before starting your day (e.g., 7:00 to 7:30 a.m.), set the tone for the day with clarity and calmness, ensuring you feel refreshed and focused. Options:

- Practice mindfulness or meditation.
- Go for a brisk walk or light jog.
- Enjoy a slow, quiet breakfast while reading or journaling.

Exercise 2: Midday Recharge (30 Minutes)

During your lunch break (e.g., 12:00 to 12:30 p.m.), break up the day's work demands, allowing yourself to regain energy and focus. Options:

- Step outside and soak in the natural environment.
- Listen to an inspiring podcast or audiobook.
- Engage in a quick creative activity like sketching or writing.

Exercise 3: Evening Reflection (60 Minutes)

After work or before bed (e.g., 8:00 to 9:00 p.m.), wind down from the day, transition to relaxation, and recharge for the next day. Options:
- Read a book purely for enjoyment.
- Watch an episode of your favorite series.
- Take a warm bath or do a calming yoga routine.

Exercise 4: Weekend Indulgence (2-Hour Block)

Pick an extended time slot on Saturday or Sunday when you can focus on activities that bring you joy and fulfillment. Options:
- Treat yourself to a long walk in nature or a bike ride.
- Explore a hobby or passion project.
- Plan an outing with friends or family that is purely for fun.

Exercise 5: Daily Self-Assessment Exercise (5 Minutes)

At the end of the day (e.g., 9:30 p.m.), check in with yourself to ensure you're consistently building a time-affluent mindset. Reflect:
- Did I dedicate at least 2 hours to myself today?
- How did I feel during my free time—relaxed, energized, or fulfilled?
- What can I adjust tomorrow to prioritize my well-being even more?

EXERCISES FOR STEP 5

Create a Customized Time Budget

Incorporate these exercises into your routine to develop a personalized time budget. Start by tracking your time, identifying priorities, and gradually aligning your daily activities with what matters most to you.

Exercise 1: Identify Your Time Wasters (Daily Reflection)

To build awareness of your current habits and pinpoint areas for improvement, at the end of each day, spend 15 minutes reviewing how you spent your time. Identify at least two activities that didn't add value or align with your goals. Examples: Excessive scrolling on social media, overthinking, or attending unproductive meetings. Write down what you could have done differently to better use that time.

Exercise 2: Track Your Time (One-Week Challenge)

To gain a clear picture of where your time is going and identify areas to optimize, for one week use a journal, spreadsheet, or time-tracking app to log your daily activities. Record how long you spend on work, personal tasks, leisure, and distractions. At the end of the week, analyze the data to determine how much time was spent on high-priority versus low-value activities.

Exercise 3: Define Your Nonnegotiables (Weekly Planning)

To prioritize what truly matters and ensure your most important tasks are scheduled, once a week spend 30 minutes to develop a plan for the upcoming week. List your essential activities, such as work, family commitments, exercise, and self-care. Identify which tasks are nonnegotiable and allocate time for them first. Highlight the most important personal or professional goals you want to accomplish.

Exercise 4: Build Your Daily Time Budget (Time-Blocking)

To create structure in your day and balance productivity with personal well-being, spend 15 minutes at the start of the day to plan it out. Divide your day into time blocks and assign specific activities or categories to each block, for example, 8:00 to 9:00 a.m. for focused work, 1:00 to 1:30 p.m. for lunch, 6:00 to 7:00 p.m. for family time. Don't forget to include recharge blocks where you focus solely on relaxation or hobbies.

Exercise 5: Evaluate and Adjust (Weekly Reflection)

To fine-tune your time management strategy and improve balance and efficiency, at the end of each week, allot 30 minutes to reflect on how well you followed your time budget. Ask yourself:
- Did I stick to my planned schedule?
- What challenges or distractions threw me off track?
- What worked well, and what needs adjustment?

Update your budget for the following week based on these insights.

Exercise 6: Create a Wasted Time Recovery Plan

Gradually eliminate distractions and build habits that align with your goals by periodically identifying one specific time-wasting habit—for example, checking social media too frequently. Develop a concrete plan to replace that habit with a productive or enjoyable activity; for instance, replace scrolling with a short walk or reading a chapter of a book. Set a reminder or use tools like app timers to keep yourself accountable.

EXERCISES FOR STEP 6
Be Mindful of Your Minutes

Being intentional how you spend time begins with awareness. These exercises are meant to help you shift from feeling time-starved to feeling in control by being mindful of your minutes.

Exercise 1: Reframing Time Scarcity

Shifting your mindset from scarcity to abundance encourages proactive and intentional use of time. If you need help, try this process:

1. Write down three common thoughts you have or phrases you say about time. Example: "I never have enough time."
2. Reframe each thought into a positive, time-abundant perspective: Example: "I never have enough time" becomes "I have enough time to do the things that matter most."
3. Repeat these reframed statements daily to cultivate a mindset of abundance.

Exercise 2: Timed Single-Tasking

Practice single-tasking by choosing one important task for the day. Set a timer for 30 to 50 minutes to focus solely on that task without switching to others. Afterward, reflect: Did focusing on one task improve your efficiency or reduce stress? How did it compare to multitasking?

Exercise 3: The "Pause and Ask" Technique

To ensure your time is directed toward meaningful and high-impact activities, before starting any task, pause and ask yourself: Is this the best use of my time right now? Will this activity bring me closer to my goals? If the answer is no, reevaluate and reprioritize.

Exercise 4: Declutter Your Commitments

Simplifying your commitments reduces overwhelm and frees time for what truly matters. Make a list of all current obligations (e.g., meetings, projects, social commitments). For each item, ask: Does this align with my top priorities? And can I delegate or eliminate this task? Adjust your schedule to reflect your true priorities.

Exercise 5: The Gratitude Log for Time

Practicing gratitude for how you use your minutes builds a positive association with time and encourages mindful choices. At the end of each day, write down three ways you spent your time that felt meaningful or productive. Reflect on why those moments were valuable to you.

EXERCISES FOR STEP 7
Be Respectful of Others' Time

These exercises will help you internalize the value of respecting others' time while cultivating habits that enhance punctuality and patience.

Exercise 1: Time Commitment Self-Audit

To assess your own habits and identify areas for improvement in respecting others' time, reflect on your punctuality over the past week. How often were you on time? Were there any instances where you kept someone waiting? Why? Write down two specific ways you can improve your punctuality or time management.

Exercise 2: Role-Reversal Reflection

To foster empathy and reinforce the importance of respecting others' schedules, recall a time when someone kept you waiting. How did it make you feel? Did it impact your impression of that person? Now, think of a time when you were late. Consider how it might have affected the other person.

Exercise 3: Time-Respect Pledge

To make a conscious commitment to valuing others' time, write a personal pledge about respecting others' time. For example: "I will honor appointments by being on time or notifying others if I'm delayed" or "I will consider how my actions impact others' schedules." Place the pledge where you'll see it daily (e.g., your desk or planner).

Exercise 4: Time-Respect Role Model

To learn from positive examples and implement respectful time habits, think of someone in your life who consistently demonstrates respect for others' time. List three behaviors or habits they practice (e.g., punctuality, clear communication about delays). Choose one of these behaviors to adopt for yourself.

EXERCISES FOR STEP 8
Create a Daily Routine

Establishing a daily routine does not mean locking yourself into a rigid schedule. It means creating a rhythm that supports your goals and well-being. These exercises are meant to help you design a routine that energizes you, fits your lifestyle, and evolves around your needs.

Exercise 1: Reflect on Your Current Routine

What tasks or habits currently dominate your day? Make a list. For each item, indicate whether it energizes or drains you. For example:

- Morning email check: Drains me. I get overwhelmed before I've even had coffee.
- Midafternoon walk: Energizes me. Clears my head, lifts my mood.
- Evening social media scroll: Drains me. I lose time and feel less focused.
- Evening journaling: Energizes me. Helps me process the day and sleep better.

Exercise 2: Design a Flexible Routine

List three daily activities and assign each a flexible window of time, such as:

- Creative writing: Between 8:30 and 10:30 a.m.
- Lunch and light walk: Any time from 12:00 to 1:30 p.m.
- Emails and admin: Between 3:00 and 4:30 p.m.
- Exercise: Between 6:00 and 8:00 a.m.
- Family time: Any time after 5:30 p.m.
- Reading or learning: Between 8:00 and 9:00 p.m.

Exercise 3: Build in Dynamic Habits

Add one energizing short-term goal or variety switch to your routine this week. For example:

- Short-term goal: Meditate for 10 minutes before bed every night for a week.
- Short-term goal: Wake up 30 minutes earlier to stretch and plan the day.
- Variety switch: Try a new recipe every other day instead of eating out.
- Variety switch: Work from a coffee shop instead of home twice this week.

EXERCISES FOR STEP 9
Plan Your Day the Night Before

These exercises will help you adopt a proactive approach to daily planning, reduce stress, and boost your productivity by starting each day with clarity and purpose.

Exercise 1: Identify Your Planning Style

To assess your planning tendencies and identify areas for improvement, reflect on whether your current approach to planning resembles Pamela's (proactive) or Nikki's (reactive). (Revisit Step 9 if you need a reminder.) How does your current style affect your productivity and stress levels? What would you like to improve about your planning habits? Commit to one small change in your planning routine for the next week.

Exercise 2: Create a Framework for Your Day

To provide structure for your day and prioritize tasks effectively, each evening, draft a simple outline of your next day. For instance:
- Morning: What will you focus on during the first hour?
- Midday: What tasks need your attention before lunch?
- Afternoon: How will you tackle important projects in the afternoon?

Be sure to include buffers for unexpected delays or interruptions.

Exercise 3: Visualization Practice

To strengthen your focus and commitment to completing your tasks, after you write down your goals for the following day, take a moment to visualize yourself accomplishing them. How will you feel once they're completed? What benefits will this bring to your day overall? Reflect on whether this visualization motivates you to follow through on your plans.

Exercise 4: Overcoming Planning Challenges

If planning habits feel overwhelming or unnatural, ease into them by writing down just one or two key tasks to complete the next day. Use a sticky note or digital reminder to keep them visible. As planning becomes more natural, gradually increase the number of tasks.

Exercise 5: Health-Priority Checklist

To ensure that your daily plans include self-care for sustained energy and clarity, ensure that each evening you plan at least one activity for the next day that supports your physical and mental well-being, such as a 10-minute walk, a balanced meal or healthy snack, or a short meditation or breathing exercise. Track how incorporating health-focused activities improves your productivity and focus.

Exercise 6: Planning Affirmation

To build confidence and enthusiasm for making planning a consistent part of your routine, create a simple affirmation to repeat each day while planning: "I am setting myself up for success by preparing for tomorrow" or "Planning tonight will give me clarity and focus in the morning." Note whether this affirmation helps you feel more positive about your planning.

EXERCISES FOR STEP 10
Integrate Habit Stacking into Your Life

Habit stacking is a simple yet powerful way to link a new habit to something you already do consistently. These exercises may help you build routines that stick by anchoring new behaviors to existing ones.

Exercise 1: Identify Anchor Habits

Make a list of ten things you already do every day without thinking—these are your anchor habits. Examples include brushing your teeth, making coffee, checking your phone, and locking the door.

Next, pick one anchor habit and choose a simple new habit to pair with it. For example:

- Anchor habit: Brushing your teeth
- New habit: Writing one thing in your gratitude journal immediately after

Exercise 2: Build a Habit Stack Routine

Pick a specific time of day (e.g., morning, lunch break, bedtime) and create a three-step habit stack that takes less than 10 minutes.

Use this format: After [CURRENT HABIT], I will [NEW HABIT].

Example morning stack:

- After I turn off my alarm, I will drink a glass of water.
- After I drink water, I will stretch for 1 minute.
- After I stretch, I will write down one thing I'm grateful for.

Repeat your habit stack daily for the next seven days and track your consistency.

Exercise 3: Troubleshoot and Rebuild

After one week of practicing your habit stack, reflect on what worked and what didn't:

- Which part of the stack felt easiest to follow?
- Where did you tend to skip steps?
- Did your anchor habit happen reliably each day?

Make adjustments as needed and rebuild your stack for week two.

EXERCISES FOR STEP 11
Create a Daily To-Do List

A well-crafted daily to-do list will help you set realistic goals about what you can accomplish. The following exercises will guide you in building lists that support your goals without overwhelming you.

Exercise 1: Craft Your Perfect To-Do List

To create your daily to-do list, grab a notebook or legal pad, or open your phone's Notes section. Write down at least five tasks you need to complete today. These could range from work commitments to personal errands. For each task, assign the amount of time it will take (even if it's a rough estimate) and a due date, if applicable; this will help keep your daily list realistic.

As you work through the list, check off completed tasks. Reflect on how it feels to accomplish each item!

Exercise 2: Prioritize Your Must-Do List

Not all tasks are created equal—that's where must-do and intend-to-do sections come in. Review your daily to-do list and highlight the most urgent or important tasks. Move these highlighted tasks to a must-do section at the top of your list and set a specific deadline for each one. If a task is not urgent, place it further down your list in the intend-to-do section.

The following day, carry over any incomplete tasks from your must-do list and your intend-to-do lists. How can you improve your list-making for the next day?

Exercise 3: Underpromise and Overdeliver

To avoid feeling overwhelmed, underpromise: Write down only the tasks you are sure you can complete that day. It's okay to aim low and be realistic. As you finish each task early or have extra time, feel free to add a quick bonus task to your day.

Reflect at the end of the day: Did you feel more productive by setting manageable goals? How did it feel to exceed expectations?

EXERCISES FOR STEP 12
Create a Running To-Do List

Not all tasks need to be done today, yet they should not be forgotten. A running to-do list captures low-priority and long-term tasks in one place so that you can manage them with intention.

Exercise 1: Running To-Do List Creation

To kick-start your running to-do list, take 5 minutes to jot down tasks or projects that you want to accomplish but that don't have an immediate deadline. Divide them into two categories: projects with a deadline and low-priority projects. Keep this list handy and update it regularly.

Exercise 2: Identify Your "Stuck" Tasks

Look at your current to-do list and identify tasks that have remained undone due to missing pieces, lack of urgency, or other roadblocks. Move them to your running to-do list. Reflect on why these tasks have stalled and write down one small action you can take to move each one forward.

Exercise 3: The Three- to Six-Month Check-In

To prevent your running to-do list from becoming a procrastination trap, review it and highlight any tasks that have been there for more than three to six months. Decide whether to:

- Commit: Set a specific deadline and move it to your active to-do list.
- Delegate: Assign it to someone else or seek help.
- Delete: Acknowledge that it's no longer a priority and remove it.

Exercise 4: Your Personal Running To-Do List Rule

To make your running to-do list work for you, establish a simple rule to keep it manageable. Examples:

- Limit it to twenty items at a time to avoid overwhelm.
- Review and update it every Sunday night to stay on track.
- Commit to completing one item per week to keep progress steady.

EXERCISES FOR STEP 13

Eat That Frog!

Tackling your most difficult or most important task first thing in the morning can transform your productivity and mindset. These exercises will help you identify your "frog" and build the habit of starting your day with purpose.

Exercise 1: Reflect on Your Current Habits

Answer the following questions to assess your time management and task prioritization:

- How do you currently choose which task to start your day with?
- Do you tend to postpone difficult tasks? Why or why not?
- How does delaying challenging tasks affect your productivity and stress levels?
- How will you make the "eat that frog" method part of your daily routine?

Exercise 2: Plan to "Eat Your Frog"

Set yourself up for success by using this checklist to prepare for each day's frog the day before:

1. Identify your frog. Example: Complete a challenging budget report.
2. Schedule time for your frog first thing in the morning. Example: From 9:00 a.m. to 11:00 a.m.
3. When needed, break the frog into smaller, actionable steps. Example:
   1. Gather financial data.
   2. Outline the key sections.
   3. Draft the report.
4. Prepare your tools and materials. Example: Have necessary documents and software ready.

Note that by breaking a big frog into smaller bites, if you get to a good stopping place but your frog is too big to finish, you can carry it over to the following day more easily while still making progress.

Exercise 3: Reflect on the Process

After implementing the "eat that frog" method for a few days, reflect: Did tackling your toughest task first improve your focus and energy for the rest of the day? What was the greatest benefit of completing your frog early? Were there any challenges or temptations to avoid your frog? How did you handle them?

EXERCISES FOR STEP 14

Touch It Once!

The "touch it once" rule helps reduce wasted time and mental clutter by encouraging decisive action. These exercises will show you where you are revisiting tasks unnecessarily and how to curb that behavior.

Exercise 1: Identify Repetitive Touch Points

To spot where you're spending unnecessary time, take a few minutes to identify five tasks you tend to handle more than once—like checking emails without responding or moving the same stack of papers. Write them down and estimate how long you typically spend revisiting each. Choose one task to apply the "touch it once" rule to every day for the next week.

Exercise 2: Quick Touch Audit

At the end of the day, jot down two tasks you revisited more than once—whether physically (like moving a book) or mentally (like rereading the same email). Next to each one, write a note about what kept you from completing it in one go. When that task pops up the following day, challenge yourself to act immediately.

Exercise 3: One Task, Two Ways

Choose a common repetitive task—like clearing dishes, folding laundry, or checking texts.

- Day 1: Handle the task the usual way, even if that means revisiting it.
- Day 2: Commit to finishing it the first time you touch it.

Compare the time spent and the energy impact between the two days.

EXERCISES FOR STEP 15
The 2-Minute Rule: Do It Now!

If a task takes 2 minutes or less, do it immediately. That is the definition of the 2-minute rule. These exercises will help you spot quick wins, manage distractions, and make the most of your small moments.

Exercise 1: Identify Opportunities for Improvement

To find areas where you can apply the 2-minute rule more effectively, identify three small personal tasks you frequently delay. Then identify three small work-related tasks you tend to put off.

Exercise 2: Experiment with Sequential vs. Spaced

Experiment with two different approaches to completing your 2-minute tasks:
1. Sequential Approach: Dedicate 10 to 15 minutes to complete as many 2-minute tasks as possible. Did this approach boost your momentum?
2. Spaced Approach: Handle 2-minute tasks as they arise throughout the day. Did this cause distractions from larger projects?

Which approach worked better for you, and why?

Exercise 3: Evaluate the Downsides

While practicing the 2-minute rule, observe any challenges or drawbacks:

- Did you find yourself distracted from bigger tasks?
- Did handling multiple mini tasks in a row lead to mental fatigue?
- Did any 2-minute tasks take longer than expected?

If you answered yes to any question, decide how you'll manage that challenge in the future.

EXERCISES FOR STEP 16

Stay Focused

Focus is a skill that can be strengthened with intention and practice. These exercises will help you identify what pulls your attention and give you the tools to regain control of your time and energy.

Exercise 1: Audit Your Distractions

Take 10 minutes to reflect on the most common distractions that derail your focus during the day. Include the following:

- Tech distractions (e.g., smartphone notifications, email alerts)
- Environmental distractions (e.g., noise, clutter)
- People distractions (e.g., unplanned conversations, family interruptions)

For each category, write down one action you can take to minimize or eliminate the distraction.

Exercise 2: Single-Tasking Practice

Dedicate a 30-minute session to a single task. During this time, silence all notifications, place your phone out of reach, and use noise-canceling headphones or move to a quiet space. At the end of the session, consider how much progress you made compared to when you multitask and how you felt about staying focused for the full duration.

Exercise 3: Create a Focus Zone

Designate a specific space and time for deep work. Describe your "focus zone" in detail, including location, tools, and environment. Commit to working in this zone for two to three sessions over the coming week. After each session, evaluate your productivity and note how the zone contributed to minimizing distractions.

Exercise 4: Find Your Secret Location (Bonus Challenge)

Channel your inner hide-and-seek expert. Identify a spot where you can work without interruptions. Use it once this week and track how much you accomplish compared to working at your usual spot.

EXERCISES FOR STEP 17

Set Boundaries

Clear boundaries protect your time, energy, and well-being. The following exercises are designed to help you identify where stronger limits are needed. They have also been created to give you practical ways to communicate with confidence.

Exercise 1: Boundary Awareness Audit

Reflect on moments when you've felt overwhelmed or overcommitted. Write down five recent situations where you could have said no but didn't. How did those choices affect your productivity or well-being?

Exercise 2: Practice Saying No

Identify two scenarios this week where you can set a time boundary. Then plan and rehearse responses to politely decline, such as "I can't take that on right now, but thank you for asking" or "I'd love to help, but my schedule won't allow it at this time."

Exercise 3: Schedule Your Priorities

Block time on your calendar for essential tasks, family, and self-care. Treat these commitments as immovable appointments.

Exercise 4: Analyze Boundary Benefits

After setting a time boundary, reflect on how it impacted your stress level, focus, and relationships. Write a short journal entry to document these changes.

Exercise 5: Role-Play Scenarios

With a friend or colleague, role-play common boundary-testing situations (e.g., a last-minute work request). Write down how you will respond, and practice responding confidently and respectfully.

EXERCISES FOR STEP 18
Use Meeting Agendas

Meetings can be powerful tools—or massive time drains. These exercises will help you prepare smarter, lead better, and ensure that the meetings you attend are worth your time.

Exercise 1: Evaluate Past Meetings

Reflect on meetings you've attended or hosted in the past. Assess their effectiveness and identify areas for improvement. Consider:
- Was there an agenda?
- Did the meeting stay on track?
- How much time was wasted?
- What were your key time management takeaways?

Exercise 2: Create a Pre-Meeting Checklist

Before your next meeting, prepare using this checklist:
- ☐ Create and distribute an agenda
- ☐ Assign roles (e.g., notetaker)
- ☐ Allocate time for each agenda item
- ☐ Confirm meeting platform/venue details
- ☐ Prepare any required materials/documents
- ☐ Communicate expectations to attendees

Exercise 3: Write a Sample Agenda

Draft an agenda for a meeting you plan to host or participate in. Use the structure below:

AGENDA
    Meeting Name: _____
    Date and Time: _____
    Location/Platform: _____

1. Welcome and Objectives (5 minutes)
2. Review Previous Meeting Minutes (5 minutes)
3. Main Agenda Items (Time Allocated)
    Topic 1: _____
    Topic 2: _____
    Topic 3: _____
4. Action Items and Next Steps (5 minutes)
5. Confirm Next Meeting Date and Adjourn (5 minutes)

Exercise 4: Practice Steering a Meeting

Meetings can get derailed for various reasons. Consider how you would address the following challenges during a meeting:
- Off-topic discussion
- Dominating participants
- Technical difficulties
- Disputes or conflicts
- Late arrivals

Exercise 5: Self-Assessment After the Meeting

After hosting or attending a meeting, evaluate its success. On a scale of 1 to 10 (with 10 being the best), assess each of the following and make any notes about what worked or what to try next time:

- Agenda effectiveness
- Time management
- Engagement from all participants
- Handling of disruptions
- Overall productivity

Exercise 6: Minute Master Bonus: Attendee Preparation Challenge

When you're invited to a meeting, practice this key question: "What may I do to prepare for the meeting?" Write down your preparation steps for an upcoming meeting.

EXERCISES FOR STEP 19

Stop Time-Leaking Conversations

By learning how to recognize and manage time-leaking conversations, you can protect your time and maintain positive relationships without sacrificing your schedule. Use the following exercises to sharpen your ability to handle time-leaking conversations with finesse.

Exercise 1: Recognize Time-Leaking Conversations

The first step to stopping time-leaking conversations is to identify them. Reflect on your past week and write down examples of conversations that may have leaked time. Answer these questions for each:

- Did the conversation meander without a clear goal or conclusion?
- Was there an overload of irrelevant details or "TMI"?
- Could the topic have been handled in a brief email or message?
- Was the conversation disruptive to your workflow?
- Did someone monopolize the conversation without providing actionable outcomes?

If you answered yes to one or more, you were probably in a time-leaking conversation.

Exercise 2: Preempt the Request

To prevent unnecessary interruptions, set clear time boundaries before conversations begin. This helps keep conversations focused and respectful of your time.

Identify a conversation that's likely to occur soon, such as a coworker who tends to chat for long periods or one who likes to "just drop by." Plan to set a clear time boundary by saying something like "I have 15 minutes before my next task—let's make the most of it" or "I'm in the middle of a task, but I can chat for 10 minutes." You might even write down your sentence and rehearse it in your mind.

After putting your boundary in action, reflect on how it felt to set that boundary. Was it difficult? How could you refine it for better delivery next time?

Exercise 3: Drive Toward a Close

To wrap up conversations without sounding abrupt, practice steering the discussion to a conclusion. Develop a few statements that acknowledge the time and help cue the close: "We've covered the main topics; let's summarize our action items before we conclude" or "I have another commitment starting soon; let's wrap this up in the next few minutes."

Reflect on past conversations where you could have used this approach. Then, practice redirecting a conversation with this summary technique. You can even role-play with a partner or in the mirror. Make sure your tone is polite and firm, not dismissive.

Exercise 4: Perfect the Art of Interruptions

Learning how to intervene politely but firmly can help you regain control of a conversation without creating discomfort. When a conversation starts to spiral, use subtle cues to steer it back. Use body language cues like shifting your posture or glancing at your watch. If that doesn't work, practice a tactful interruption: "That's an interesting point, but let's return to our main topic to stay on track" or "I appreciate your insights; may I share my perspective on this?"

Think of a past conversation where you wished you had interrupted. Write out how you would have interrupted to steer the discussion back on track. Then role-play the interruption with a partner, practicing it with confidence and respect.

Exercise 5: Have a Catchphrase Ready

Sometimes you need to step up your boundaries when conversations persist longer than desired. To exit conversations without feeling guilty or awkward, prepare two or three catchphrases—polite yet firm lines to help exit a conversation, such as: "I'd love to continue this, but I need to return to my project to meet its deadlines" or "This has been a great discussion, but I have a meeting starting shortly."

Test out your catchphrases in real conversations—even if they're not time-leaking conversations. Notice how it feels to assert your boundaries with confidence.

Exercise 6: Use Physical Signals

Setting clear physical boundaries can reinforce your time management and protect your focus. Practice using physical signals like wearing headphones or setting a Do Not Disturb sign in your workspace during deep work sessions.

Think of a scenario where this could be useful, such as in an open office or during a long meeting. Then, reflect on your comfort level with these methods. How can you make them seem polite yet effective?

EXERCISES FOR STEP 20
Minimize Wait Time

Waiting is often unavoidable; however, wasted time is not. These exercises will help you track, assess, and reduce wait times so your days run more efficiently.

Exercise 1: Track and Reflect

Take a week to monitor how much time you spend waiting in various situations. How long did each wait last? Could it have been avoided? What could you do differently next time to reduce your wait? What surprised you most about your current waiting habits?

Exercise 2: Apply the Tips

Pick one of this step's tips for minimizing wait times. Experiment with it for a week and note your experiences. Would you use that approach again? How will you continue to minimize wait times in the future?

Exercise 3: Group Engagement During Waits

The next time you're waiting for an event or appointment in a group setting, engage with those around you. Afterward, reflect on the experience: What activity or topic did you use to engage the group? Did the wait time feel shorter? Why or why not?

EXERCISES FOR STEP 21

Leverage Dead Time

Dead time happens. If you know how to manage it, "dead" time does not have to be unproductive time. These exercises have been designed to share how you can turn idle moments into your most productive time.

Exercise 1: Assess Your Dead Time

Take a week to track moments of dead time in your daily routine. Each day, jot down when and where these moments occur, what you were doing, how long they lasted, and how you could have used the time more intentionally.

Exercise 2: Identify Your Time Transformation Tools

Think of common dead-time scenarios you face, such as commuting, waiting in lines, or sitting in appointments. For each one, come up with a tool or strategy you could use to make that time productive or meaningful. Note why each strategy would work for you. For example: "During my commute, I could listen to audiobooks because it helps me absorb new ideas without needing a screen."

Exercise 3: Experiment and Reflect

For the next week, commit to trying at least one new strategy each day during a moment of dead time. At the end of each day, reflect: What strategy did you use? How did it go? Would you use it again?

Exercise 4: Strategize Your Week

Look ahead at the upcoming week. For each day, identify at least one moment when you're likely to encounter dead time. Then, decide in advance how you'll use that time more intentionally, and list any resources (apps, headphones, notebook, and so on) you'll need.

Exercise 5: Brainstorm a Creative Project

Think of three creative projects you've been putting off—such as writing a short story, launching a business idea, or outlining a personal goal. Choose one and spend 5 minutes of dead time each day brainstorming the first steps toward starting it.

Exercise 6: Gratitude on the Go

Use idle moments to practice gratitude. Any time you're waiting in line, in traffic, or between meetings, take a moment to think of three things you're grateful for and, if possible, jot them down.

Exercise 7: Evaluate the Week

After a week of transforming dead time into "alive" time, reflect on the experience: How much dead time did you successfully convert? What worked best for you? What will you keep doing moving forward?

EXERCISES FOR STEP 22

Use Digital Technology to Your Advantage

The right tech tools can become time-saving allies rather than digital distractions. These exercises are meant to help you identify ways to streamline your tasks and free up your time for what matters.

Exercise 1: Optimize Email Management

For the next week, try one of these email strategies:

- Set up email filters to categorize messages automatically.
- Use canned responses for frequently asked questions.

At the end of the week, reflect: How much time did you save? Was email less stressful to manage?

Exercise 2: Repetitive Task Inventory

Identify areas in your personal and professional life where streamlining or automation could free up time. List five repetitive tasks you perform daily—such as making coffee or sorting emails. For each task, research and list one tool, app, or device that could streamline or automate it. Write down the estimated time you would save weekly.

Example:

- Task: Paying bills manually.
- Tool: Prism App.
- Time saved: 1 hour per week.

Exercise 3: Trial Run of Streamlining/Automation Tools

It's important to test new streamlining and automation tools to make sure they work for you—and to allow yourself time to get used to them before you decide they do or don't. To test new tools:

1. Choose one task from your repetitive task inventory.
2. Implement a streamlining/automation tool for this task.
3. Use the tool for one week and then assess: How easy was it to set up? How much time did you save? Were there any challenges or adjustments needed?

Exercise 4: Time Gained Reflection

After streamlining or automating at least three tasks, calculate the total hours saved over a week. Write down how you will reinvest this time over the next week—perhaps learning a new skill or spending quality time with loved ones. At the end of the week, evaluate whether the time was used effectively and how you felt about it.

Exercise 5: Creative Balance Check

To help keep balance between technology and personal connection or creativity, identify tasks that should *not* be automated. List five tasks that require your personal touch—such as brainstorming for work or family conversations—and reflect on why those tasks are best left unautomated. Then, commit to dedicating uninterrupted time to those tasks each week.

EXERCISES FOR STEP 23
Minimize Decision Fatigue

Making decisions is a natural part of life, but when faced with too many choices, it can become mentally exhausting. Use the following exercises to learn how to streamline your decision-making process and minimize decision fatigue so that you can focus on what truly matters.

Exercise 1: Track Your Daily Decisions

The first step to reducing decision fatigue is recognizing how many decisions you make each day. For one week, track your decisions. Start from the moment you wake up and note every significant decision you make (e.g., breakfast choice, what to wear, how to allocate your time).

At the end of each day, reflect on the frequency and types of decisions you've made. Analyze which decisions felt mentally draining and which ones were simple. Were there decisions that could have been streamlined or made automatically?

Exercise 2: Create a Routine for the First Hour of Your Day

Start your day with fewer decisions by establishing a morning routine. A predictable routine helps you minimize mental strain early in the day.

1. Write down your ideal morning routine. What activities would you do consistently every day to avoid wasting energy on decisions? For example:
   - Wake up at 6:00 am.
   - Drink a glass of water.
   - Spend 10 minutes stretching or meditating.
   - Eat the same breakfast each day.
2. Try it for one week, keeping the routine simple and repeatable.
3. Reflect: How did this routine affect your energy and decision-making throughout the day?

Exercise 3: Implement a Weekly Meal Plan

Food decisions can be a huge drain on your time and mental energy. Instead of deciding what to eat each day, create a weekly meal plan.

1. Plan your meals for the week. Choose simple meals that you can repeat regularly (e.g., Taco Tuesdays, Salad Thursdays).
2. Shop for all the ingredients you need for the entire week.
3. Stick to the plan for at least one week, adjusting if necessary.
4. Evaluate the impact: Did having a set plan save you time? Did it make meal prep easier?

Exercise 4: Use If-Then Rules for Smaller Decisions

Use if-then rules to simplify decision-making and make quicker choices without overthinking. This approach helps you automate choices and reduce decision fatigue.

1. Write down at least five small decisions you face regularly (e.g., what to wear, where to work, when to check email).
2. For each, create an if-then rule:
   - IF I need to decide on an outfit quickly, THEN I'll default to one of three go-to outfits.
   - IF I'm deciding what time to schedule a meeting, THEN I'll pick 10:00 a.m. every time.
3. Apply these rules for the next week and note how much easier decision-making becomes.

Exercise 5: Establish Hard Edges to Your Day

To minimize decisions about when to stop or start activities, create clear boundaries between your work and personal time, and between activities during your day. Not only will this help you avoid decision fatigue, but it will help avoid overwork and mental exhaustion.

First, define your workday boundaries. For example, set a hard end time for work (e.g., 5:00 p.m.) and stick to it. Then, schedule nonnegotiable time for personal activities, such as dinner with family or time for relaxation.

Test this for one week and observe at the end of each workday how having hard edges to your day helps you focus and minimize decision-making.

EXERCISES FOR STEP 24

Declutter Your Space

Below are decluttering exercises to help you transform your space and your mindset. By incorporating them into your daily routine, you'll not only reclaim your physical space but also experience the mental clarity that comes with a decluttered life.

Exercise 1: Clutter Reality Check

Spend 10 minutes surveying your environment and answering the following questions:

- What is the most cluttered area in your space (such as desk, closet, or junk drawer)?
- How does this clutter make you feel? Stressed, distracted, indifferent, or something else?
- What is one item in that space you know you don't need but haven't let go of yet?

Action Step: Remove one nonessential item from that area and either donate, recycle, or discard it.

Exercise 2: The "One In, One Out" Rule

For one week, commit to this challenge: Every time you bring a new item into your space—whether clothes, books, gadgets, or something else—remove one item you no longer need. At the end of the week, assess how this simple habit has impacted your space and your mindset.

Exercise 3: 60-Second Decluttering Blitz

Set a timer for 1 minute and declutter one small area. Suggestions:
- Your desk: Clear away old papers, pens that don't work, or forgotten coffee mugs.
- Your bag: Remove old receipts and items you no longer use.
- Your email inbox: Delete spam, or archive messages you've already read.

Reflect: Was it easier or harder than you expected?

Exercise 4: The Sentimental Box

Find a box and label it Sentimental Items. Over the next month, place items you're unsure about keeping into this box. At the end of the month, revisit the box. If you didn't miss the items, it might be time to let them go.

Exercise 5: Decluttering Buddy System

Partner with a friend or family member to tackle clutter together. Spend 30 minutes decluttering each person's space together. Offer each other an honest, supportive perspective on what to keep and what to let go of. Celebrate your progress with a clutter-free coffee break!

EXERCISES FOR STEP 25

Streamline Your Dressing Routine

Below are interactive exercises to simplify your morning routine, reduce stress, and reclaim precious minutes.

Exercise 1: Morning Routine Timer

Tomorrow morning, time yourself as you get dressed—from start to finish, including grooming and accessorizing. Compare your time to the Marks and Spencer average of 17 minutes. Which part of your process takes the longest? Identify one area to streamline, such as choosing an outfit, finding accessories, or putting on shoes.

Exercise 2: Closet Audit Challenge

Dedicate 30 minutes to assessing your wardrobe using the following checklist:
- Identify items you haven't worn in the past year.
- Categorize them into three piles: Keep, Donate, and Maybe.
- Place the Maybe pile in a box. Revisit it in six months. If you haven't missed anything, donate the box.

Bonus: Share a photo of your decluttered closet with a friend or family member as a motivational checkpoint.

Exercise 3: Outfit Planning Sprint

Spend 20 minutes creating five grab-and-go outfits for work or casual wear. Match tops, bottoms, and accessories, and hang them together in your closet. Label these outfits with tags like Monday, Casual Friday, or Date Night.

Pro Tip: Take photos of these outfits to use as a quick reference on busy mornings.

Exercise 4: Dress Rehearsal Weekend

Set aside a weekend afternoon to try on outfits you haven't worn in a while. Experiment with new combinations of tops, bottoms, and accessories. Take note of what works and what doesn't. Store the successful combinations in the grab-and-go section of your closet. Outcome: A refreshed wardrobe without buying anything new!

Exercise 5: Seasonal Wardrobe Swap

Spend 15 minutes categorizing your clothing by season. Store out-of-season items in bins or at the back of your closet. Leave only the current season's wardrobe accessible. Notice how much easier it is to find what you need when your closet is less cluttered.

Exercise 6: Accessory Speed Test

Challenge yourself to choose accessories in under 2 minutes: Select one necklace or tie, one pair of earrings or cufflinks, and one watch or bracelet. To avoid overthinking, limit your choices to five to ten versatile accessories.

Pro Tip: Keep accessories in a designated spot for quick access.

Exercise 7: "Sizeless" Outfit Prep

Identify at least one set of clothes—a pair of pants and a shirt, a skirt and blouse, a dress—that feels comfortable regardless of daily physical fluctuations. Place these items in your grab-and-go section for days when comfort is key.

Bonus Tip: Pair these with slip-on shoes to save even more time.

Exercise 8: Digital Outfit Planner

Download a wardrobe planning app or create an album on your phone. Take photos of ten favorite outfits and organize them into categories like Work, Casual, or Formal. Use this digital planner to simplify your morning decisions.

EXERCISES FOR STEP 26
Turn Off Default Notifications

Your phone is designed to get your attention. Remember, however, that your time belongs to *you*! These exercises have been created to help you tame the constant beeping of notifications.

Exercise 1: Do Not Disturb Challenge

For one week, activate Do Not Disturb mode during your work or focus hours. At the end of the week, consider: Did you notice fewer interruptions? How did this impact your focus and productivity? Will you continue using this feature?

Exercise 2: Customize Priority Notifications

Identify up to five apps where notifications are critical. Adjust settings to allow only time-sensitive notifications and set custom alert tones for priority messages. After testing the customization for a week, consider: Were you able to distinguish important alerts from distractions? Did this reduce the overall noise from your device?

Exercise 3: Practice the Mute Technique

Choose one group chat or email thread to mute for 24 hours. Before muting, consider: How often do notifications from this thread interrupt you? After muting, review: How did you feel with fewer interruptions? Decide if muting this channel permanently would benefit your focus.

Exercise 4: Celebrate Digital Wins

At the end of a month, reward yourself for taking control of your notifications. Go out for coffee. Or take a notification-free nature walk. While doing so, consider: How has this habit improved your productivity and stress levels?

EXERCISES FOR STEP 27

Unplug from Technology

Being connected to your tech tools 24/7 does not equate to being present. These exercises are meant to help you step away from your screen and reconnect with yourself, your family, your friends, and the world around you.

Exercise 1: Simple Digital Detox

Try this simple one-day digital detox. It's nothing extreme—just enough to feel the benefits:

Morning (Wake-Up to Noon)

- No phone or screens for the first hour after you wake up. Instead, journal, stretch, go outside, or enjoy a quiet breakfast.
- Turn off nonessential notifications for the day. Allow texts and calls from important people only.
- Check your devices just *once* midmorning (and only if needed) then put them away.

Afternoon (Noon to 6:00 p.m.)

- Keep your phone on silent or in another room while you work, read, or enjoy your activities.
- Replace scroll breaks with an offline activity:
  - Walk around
  - Do a few stretches
  - Doodle or sketch
  - Make tea or coffee slowly
- If you must be online for work, limit it to scheduled blocks, such as 30 minutes online, then a 5-minute break offline.

Evening (6:00 p.m. to Bedtime)
- No social media or news after dinner.
- Unwind with offline activities:
  - Read a book
  - Take a bath
  - Play a board game or card game
  - Call or meet a friend
- Turn off all screens at least 1 hour before bed. Use this time for quiet reflection, journaling, meditation, or planning the next day.

Bonus Tip: If possible, use a basic alarm clock so you don't need your phone in the bedroom at all.

EXERCISES FOR STEP 28
Set Tech-Free Zones at Home and at Work

These exercises help you implement and sustain tech-free zones, enhancing your ability to focus, relax, and connect with others. Start small, track your progress, and celebrate the freedom that tech-free zones can bring!

Exercise 1: Audit Your Current Tech Habits

Track your phone usage for one day using a screen-time app. Record how often you check your device and in which environments (e.g., during meals, during walks, or while working). Reflect on whether these habits are aligned with your goals for time affluence and productivity.

Exercise 2: Introduce Family or Team Challenges

Engage others in creating shared tech-free zones: Set a specific time (e.g., during dinner or meetings) when everyone agrees to leave devices in a designated area. Then reward consistency with simple incentives, like a family game night or a team coffee break. Reflect: How did this collective commitment affect the quality of interaction or focus?

Exercise 3: Low-Tech Meal Experiences

Try a dining experiment: At your next meal, have everyone place their phones in a basket or in another room. Use conversation prompts like "What was the highlight of your day?" or "What's one thing you're grateful for?" Afterward, reflect: Did the food taste better? Was the conversation more engaging?

Exercise 4: Walk Without Tech

Take a 20-minute walk, leaving your phone at home (or in your pocket on silent mode). Pay attention to your surroundings—the sounds, sights, and smells. Afterward, journal your experience: Did you feel more relaxed or focused after this tech-free activity?

Exercise 5: Tech-Free Worktime

Dedicate part of your workday to deep focus by placing your phone in another room or in a drawer. Set a timer for 25 to 50 minutes of uninterrupted work. Use breaks to check your phone *briefly* before resuming focus.

Exercise 6: Weekly Digital Detox Day

Choose one day per week to go tech-free for at least 4 to 6 hours. Plan offline activities in advance, such as visiting a museum, hiking, or spending time with loved ones. Reflect on how this break impacts your stress levels and sense of time affluence.

Exercise 7: Reward Yourself

If you successfully implement tech-free zones for a week, treat yourself to a favorite meal, a new book, or extra leisure time. Use the reward as positive reinforcement to continue the habit.

EXERCISES FOR STEP 29
Learn to Deal with Setbacks

Setbacks are part of any meaningful journey. The are not signs of failure. These exercises are meant to help you reframe stumbles as stepping stones so that you can better regain your momentum with purpose.

Exercise 1: Revisit Your Goals and Strategies

Here are two options that might help you reconnect to your goals, and strategies to reach them:

The *Why* Reconnection Drill: Reconnect to your deeper motivation—beyond just deadlines or productivity. Take 10 minutes to write down why your goal matters. Ask: What do I hope to feel, do, or become once I reach this goal?

Reality-Check Mapping: Draw two quick timelines: one showing your ideal progress toward your goal, and one showing what actually happened. Then ask: Where did things diverge, and what can I learn from that?

Exercise 2: Start Small to Regain Momentum

Here are two options to try when you need to get back on track:

The 5-Minute Action Challenge: Choose one micro-task you've been avoiding. Set a timer for just 5 minutes. Start the task, without pressure to finish. Reflect: Did starting change your mindset?

The Two-Task Reset: Pick only two essential tasks for the following day, and write them down. Commit to finishing them no matter what. Cross them off and reflect on how it felt to reclaim some control.

Exercise 3: Adjust Your Strategies

Try one of the following approaches to determine where adjustments are needed:

A Flexibility Audit: Ask yourself: Where have I been too rigid? Where could I build in breathing room or make my expectations more realistic? Then, make one small adjustment to your next plan or schedule.

A Strategy Swap: Choose a task that consistently causes friction. Brainstorm three alternate ways to approach it—for instance, do it at a different time, break it up, delegate it. Try one variation this week and track how it affects your flow.

EXERCISES FOR STEP 30

Be Available for What (and Who) Matters Most

Time affluence is not merely about getting more done. It is about being more present for what matters. These exercises are meant to help you focus your energy on the people and passions that will give you the life you want.

Exercise 1: Who Grounds You?

Grab a pen and jot down the names of three people who make you feel more like yourself—people who lift you up and help you breathe easier. When was the last time you connected with them? Now choose one and reach out to them this week. Send a voice note. Plan a walk. Share a meal. A few minutes can bring you back to who you are.

Exercise 2: What Brings You Back to Life?

List three things that bring you joy. When can you fit one of them in during the next seven days? Don't wait until your to-do list is empty or your schedule is clear. Schedule it now. Even 15 minutes makes a difference.

Notes

[1] Andy Medici, "The Workplace Mainstay Employees Want Companies to Reconsider," *The Business Journals*, November 14, 2024.

[2] Michelle Peng, "How 'Time Poverty' at Work Makes You Less Healthy," Charter (in partnership with *TIME*), March 10, 2024.

[3] Medora Lee, "Time's Money, But How Much? Here's What Americans Think an Hour of Their Time Is Worth," *USA Today*, May 1, 2024.

[4] Naval Ravikant, "Set an Aspirational Hourly Rate: Outsource Tasks That Cost Less Than Your Hourly Rate," *Naval* (blog), May 1, 2019.

[5] Alison Overholt, "The Art of Multitasking," *Fast Company*, September 30, 2002.

[6] Christopher M. Barnes, "The Ideal Work Schedule, as Determined by Circadian Rhythms," *Harvard Business Review*, January 28, 2015.

[7] Lev Grossman, "Runner-Up: Tim Cook, the Technologist," *TIME*, December 19, 2012.

[8] Max Alberhasky, PhD, "How Much Free Time Do You Need to Be Happy," *Psychology Today*, March 13, 2023.

[9] Shlomo Sprung, "LinkedIn CEO Jeff Weiner Shares Insights on Leadership," *Business Insider*, September 7, 2012.

[10] TrackingTime, "Build a Productive Workflow Using Day Theming," TrackingTime website, December 10, 2024.

[11] Tanja Trkulja, "Effects of Workplace Distractions: Crucial Statistics," Clockify website, July 25, 2024.

[12] Rob Marvin, "Americans Spend Over 11 Hours Per Day Consuming Media," *PCMag*, July 31, 2018.

[13] Simon Kemp, "Digital 2021: Global Overview Report," DataReportal, January 27, 2021.

[14] Caroline Castrillon, "How to Manage Email Overload At Work," *Forbes*, December 10, 2021.

[15] "Multitasking: Switching Costs," American Psychological Organization website, March 20, 2006.

[16] Petri Lehtonen, "The Cost of Poor Quality Meetings: A Deep Dive into the Data," Flowtrace Collaboration Diagnostics website, May 21, 2023.

[17] Kiera Abbamonte, "The 5 Best Time Tracking Apps in 2025," Zapier website, December 6, 2024.

[18] Aditi Bharade, "A Top Pepsi Exec Says He Organizes Every Hour of His Day in a Color-Coded Pie Chart and Audits It to Ensure He's Efficient," *Business Insider*, September 24, 2024.

[19] Erin E. Rupp, "Juggling Multiple Tasks: 7 Tips to Keep Everything on Track," ABLE website, November 8, 2022.

[20] Roberto P. Benzo, MD, "Toward a Realistic Approach to Mindfulness and Time Management," Mayo Clinic Connect, August 26, 2022.

[21] *Having It All: Love, Success, Sex, Money Even if You Are Starting with Nothing . . .* , Helen Gurley Brown, Pocket, 1985.

[22] Marissa Higgins, "Why You're Always Early," *Bustle*, May 16, 2016.

[23] Susan Krauss Whitbourne, "Why It's Such a Bad Idea to Keep Someone Waiting," *Psychology Today*, August 20, 2024.

[24] Christina Desmarais, "30 CEOs Reveal the Daily Habits Responsible for Their Successes," *Inc.*, September 18, 2015.

[25] Lauren Valenti, "Oprah Winfrey's 5 Rules to a Better Life," *Vogue*, January 5, 2018.

[26] Srinivas Rao, "Why Planning Your Day the Night Before Dramatically Increases Your Productivity," Medium, January 18, 2017.

[27] "How 7 Extremely Successful Leaders Use Task Lists to Achieve Goals," Oakflow website.

[28] Grace Kay and Sarah Jackson, "Jack Dorsey's Daily Routine: Meditation, a 'Wake Me Up' Lemon Drink, and 7-Minute Workouts," Yahoo! Life, February 16, 2025.

[29] Pavithra Mohan, "These 10 CEOs' Top To-Do Hacks," *Fast Company*, May 21, 2017.

[30] Sarah Lynch, "A CEO's Guide to To-Do Lists: How to Organize and Prioritize Your Tasks," *Inc.*, October 29, 2024.

[31] Andrey Fadeev, "A CEO's Routine: How To Organize and Use Your Time Wisely," *Forbes*, November 26, 2024.

[32] "The Power of the 'Touch It Once' Principle: Revolutionising Productivity," Chris Ball, *Chris Ball* (blog), June 18, 2024.

[33] Erik Sherman, "How to Hack Tony Hsieh's Email Productivity Technique," *Inc.*, August 10, 2016.

[34] Kathy Deady, "The Two-Minute Rule: What It Is and How It Works," Timely website, August 1, 2022.

[35] John Rampton, "Unleashing the Power of the Two-Minute Rule: A Productivity Hack," MSN, undated.

[36] Shana Lebowitz, "A Productivity Expert Says the 'Do It Now' Rule Will Make You More Organized Immediately," *Business Insider*, May 27, 2017.

[37] Blake Thorne, "How Distractions at Work Take Up More Time Than You Think," I Done This website, October 21, 2023.

[38] Nina Tamburello, "6 Productivity Tricks You Can Learn from CEOs," The Muse website, June 19, 2020.

[39] Emma Sim, "10 Best Time-Management Skills Practiced by Presidents and CEOs Worldwide," Study International website, April 10, 2024.

[40] Justin Bariso, "Microsoft CEO Satya Nadella's 3-Rule Method for Running Effective Meetings," *Inc.*, October 22, 2019.

[41] Tae Kim, *The Nvidia Way: Jensen Huang and the Making of a Tech Giant*, W.W. Norton & Company, 2024.

[42] "Consumer Survey: The State of Waiting in Line (2022)," Waitwhile website, June 28, 2022.

[43] Nick Mathews, "We All Hate to Wait: Research Explains Why," *The Society Pages*, December 14, 2020.

[44] Grace Cook, "12 Tips for Time Management for Successful CEOs," Plecto website, March 22, 2018.

[45] Jack Flynn, "15+ Average Commute Time Statistics [2023]: How Long Is the Average American Commute?," Zippia website, February 13, 2023.

[46] "How Much Time of an Average Life Is Spent Waiting?" Reference website, August 4, 2015.

[47] Robert Greene, *The 50th Law*, HarperCollins 2009.

[48] Robin Sharma, *The 5AM Club: Own Your Morning, Elevate Your Life*, HarperCollins, 2018.

[49] Christina Desmarais, "30 CEOs Reveal the Daily Habits Responsible for Their Success," *Inc.*, September 18, 2015.

[50] Brian Contreras, "Four Ways Top CEOs Are Making AI Work for Them," *Inc.*, September 30, 2024.

[51] Eva M. Krockow, "How Many Decisions Do We Make Each Day?" *Psychology Today*, September 27, 2018.

[52] Brian Wansink and Jeffery Sobal, "Mindless Eating: The 200 Daily Food Decisions We Overlook," *Environment and Behavior* 39, January 2007.

[53] Anne Bogel, "7 Ways I'm Minimizing Decision Fatigue in My Daily Life," *Modern Mrs. Darcy* (blog), April 16, 2018.

[54] William Worley, "Why Steve Jobs Always Wore the Same Thing," *CNN*, October 9, 2015.

[55] Diane Roberts Stoler Ed.D., "The Many Mental Benefits of Decluttering," *Psychology Today*, February 15, 2023.

[56] Tracy Lopez, "How Long Does It Take The Average Person To Get Dressed?" *Bliss Tulle* (blog), August 25, 2022.

[57] Georgette Mosbacher, *Feminine Force: Release the Power Within You to Create the Life You Deserve*, Touchstone Books, 1994.

[58] "Workplace Distractions Statistics: Problems and Solutions in 2024," TeamStage website.

[59] Jill Duffy, "Dismissing All Your Notifications? 5 Ways to Make Them Effective," *PCMag*, September 9, 2024.

[60] Steve Glaveski, "Stop Letting Push Modifications Ruin Your Productivity," *Harvard Business Review*, March 19, 2018.

[61] Karen Tiber Leland, "You Could Be Your Own Biggest Interruption. Here's How to Stop and Find Your Focus," *Inc.*, August 12, 2019.

[62] Matt Sonnen, "The Power of Silence: Turning Off Notifications Enhances Productivity," WealthManagement.com, March 25, 2024.

[63] Tatum Hunter, "Technology's Role in the 'Loneliness Epidemic,'" *Washington Post*, May 15, 2023.

[64] Risa Gells-Watnick, "Americans' Use of Mobile Technology and Home Broadband," Pew Research Center, January 31, 2024.

[65] "Digital Detox: How to Unplug and Recharge, A Step-by-Step Guide," *Keep It Glam* (blog), August 18, 2024.

[66] Alison Coleman, "Six Business Leaders Share Their Digital Detox Strategies," *Forbes*, November 27, 2018.

[67] Cara Tabachnick, "Schools Across the US Restrict Cellphones amid Growing Behavior, Mental Health, Academic Concerns," *CBS News*, September 2, 2024.

[68] Dwayne Oxford, "Why Are US States, School Districts Banning Smartphones in Schools?" *Al Jazeera*, July 6, 2024.

[69] Allison Arnold, "Should More Restaurants Ban Phones at the Table?" *Delish*, May 9, 2024.

[70] Emily Retter, "Billionaire Tech Mogul Bill Gates Reveals He Banned His Children from Mobile Phones Until They Turned 14," *Mirror*, April 20, 2017.

[71] Leander Kahney, *Tim Cook: The Genius Who Took Apple to the Next Level*, Portfolio, 2019.

[72] Anna Peel, "CEO Excellence: Time and Energy Practice," *ValueWalk*, March 15, 2022.

Resources

If you are interested in sharpening your time management skills, here are some top-rated podcasts that offer practical strategies and insights:

Before Breakfast. Hosted by Laura Vanderkam, this podcast offers practical time management tips to help listeners make the most of their mornings and enhance daily productivity.

Beyond the To-Do List. Hosted by Erik Fisher, this podcast explores productivity strategies and real-life experiences, providing insights on how to implement practical productivity techniques.

Getting Things Done. Based on David Allen's renowned methodology, this podcast delves into productivity and organization, sharing insights and strategies for managing tasks and reducing stress.

It's About Time. Hosted by Anna Dearmon Kornick, this podcast offers insights on balancing work, life, and self-care, providing time management strategies tailored for busy professionals seeking harmony.

The Mel Robbins Podcast. Hosted by Mel Robbins, this show frequently delves into strategies designed to help listeners enhance their daily routines, overcome procrastination, and build momentum through small, consistent actions.

A Productive Conversation. Hosted by productivity strategist Mike Vardy, this podcast discusses tips, tools, and tactics designed to enhance productivity, time management, and goal setting.

The Productivity Show. Presented by Asian Efficiency, this podcast provides insights into time management and productivity, offering strategies to help listeners achieve their goals efficiently.

Take Back Time. Hosted by Penny Zenker, this podcast focuses on leadership and productivity, sharing experiences and insights on practical time management to enhance efficiency and effectiveness.

The Tim Ferriss Show. Hosted by Tim Ferriss, this podcast features interviews with world-class performers, uncovering their routines and strategies for productivity and time management. This podcast offers valuable insights and strategies to help you enhance your time management skills and boost productivity.

Time Management Tips from Captain Time. Hosted by Garland Coulson, this podcast offers practical advice on time management and productivity techniques to help listeners get more done and achieve work-life balance.

The Time Tamers Podcast. Hosted by Theresa Harp, this podcast helps moms with time management and productivity strategies, enabling them to take back control of their lives.

Work + Life Harmony. Hosted by Megan Sumrell, this podcast provides practical tips on time management, organization, and productivity, aiming to help women achieve harmony between work and life.

Index

About the Author

ANN MARIE SABATH is the author of eleven books, including the best-selling *What Self-Made Millionaires Do That Most People Don't*. Her passion for productivity and investing grew from a decade spent learning the art of wealth-building under the guidance of a seasoned stock market guru. While building her financial nest egg, Sabath discovered something just as valuable as money: time affluence.

That dual insight inspired The Wannabe book series. The first title, *The Wannabe Investor: 40 Must-Know Facts Before Buying Your First Stock*, simplifies the complex world of investing for beginners. Its follow-up, *The Wannabe Minute Master: 30 Steps to Become Time Affluent*, offers readers a practical path to reclaiming their time and maximizing their daily focus.

Drawing on years of real-world discipline, strategic planning, and intentional living, Sabath empowers individuals to create success on their own terms—one smart habit at a time.